Hon. James G. Blaine.

LIFE AND PUBLIC SERVICES

OF

Hon. James G. Blaine,

THE ILLUSTRIOUS AMERICAN ORATOR, DIPLOMAT AND STATESMAN.

BY

JAMES P. BOYD, A. M.,

Author of "Life of General U. S. Grant," "Life of General William T. Sherman," "Life of General Philip H. Sheridan," etc.

WITH AN INTRODUCTION

BY HON. JOHN RUSSELL YOUNG,

President of the Union League, Philadelphia; Author of "General Grant's Tour Around the World."

ILLUSTRATED.

PUBLISHERS' UNION.

1893.

CONTENTS.

CHAPTER III.

A Teacher.

CHAPTER IV.

An Editor.

CHAPTER V.

In the Maine Legislature.

LIST OF ILLUSTRATIONS.

The attitude of Mr. Blaine at this time was a governing factor in his career. He had been in accord with the Republican party. He was its most brilliant leader, even in a group of leaders which embraced Garfield and Allison, Roscoe Conkling, and Morton, of Indiana. He was even an extreme Republican. He had taken part in the impeachment experiment against President Johnson, although in later years, as did General Grant, he regretted this impetuosity, or that he had permitted reasons of political necessity to justify such a proceeding. If he had not accepted the first nomination of Grant with enthusiasm, it was because that nomination was not welcome to Republican leaders. However, he had supported it with eloquence, loyalty and courage. There was no reason, therefore, why, had he followed the destiny of the Soldier in politics, he should not have rounded his own with the Presidency.

President Grant saw in the South a condition of affairs which could only be met by force. Lawlessness and rapine swept entire commonwealths. Southern public opinion condemned deeds of violence against political opponents. The fervid volume of Mr. Tourgee, in which he described his forlorn experiences as a Northern soldier striving to make his home in the South, may be accepted as a true picture of this unwholesome time. Grant would have suppressed disorder by force. Blaine looked upon it as an after-throbbing of the war—rebellion dying out in pain; something to be treated with infinite patience, forbearance and care. He feared that military interference, such as the President contemplated, would entail evils greater than those which it was sought to remedy. He was a man of peace. He was a statesman. He had lived under the sword—and dreaded its sinister shadow even in the hands of Grant.

History has not passed judgment as to whether Grant or Blaine was in error in regard to this proposed Force Bill. That we cannot know until the secret archives of the government, upon which the President took action, are brought to light. But Blaine was master of the House, and had his way. The Force Bill was defeated, and as a policy it was never again to be felt in American statesmanship.

This independent and intrepid action of Blaine may be regarded as the beginning of the differences with Grant, which were to forever debar him from the Presidency. Grant in his reserved, uncomplaining way, accepted the defeat in silence. But he never forgot it, and Blaine remained no longer in his confidence.

If Grant, like Jackson, had been turbulent in his resentments, he might have driven Blaine out of the party. There was nothing, however, in the attitude of the administration to disturb the relations of Blaine with the party. Had he divined subsequent antagonisms it would have been different. President Grant was serving his second term. He had declared that he would not be a candidate for re-election. His attitude towards the Republican aspirants for his seat was that of impartiality. Blaine and Conkling, Morton, Hayes and Jewell, were apparently his friends, and each alike entitled to the party confidence. His choice was Hamilton Fish, the Secretary of State; but even this preference he did not express in public. After Fish he would have preferred Conkling, but the New York Senator was young and could wait. He gave no sign. The various leaders went out to muster their forces. The convention assembled, and after a bitter contest, in which Blaine was with difficulty defeated, nominated Governor Hayes, of Ohio. When the convention was over, it was seen that the administration negatively—in silence, as it were—had defeated Blaine. It was the virtual close of his career as a candidate for the Presidency. His leadership never after was that of a leader of the party, but rather that of a powerful remnant, which was more effective in defeating the ambitions of those who had no favor in his eyes than in furthering his own.

What would have been the position of Blaine had he kept time to the music of the Grant administration would be an interesting political inquiry. It would seem to have been almost a law of his career as the most brilliant civilian in the party to follow the military star until it went down, and then take his part of its radiance. This had been the attitude of Jefferson to Washington, or, to accept a closer analogy, that of Van Buren to Jackson. There was, however, a sentiment of impatience on the part of the political leaders of the Republican party towards military men. Secretary Chase voiced this impatience when he said that military men should have military honors—rank, pensions, titles, commands; that in material things, decorations and dignities the Republic should shower them with a lavish hand. They should, however, have no part in political affairs. Their training was not conducive to statesmanship; was rather antagonistic to it. Civil duties should fall to those whose education was in civil life.

Chase, like Blaine, was obscured by the soldier. The avatar of Grant made him a Democrat. Blaine did not follow the example. He remained with the party, but ever in a position of obscuration. The best that he could do was to interrupt the careers of Morton and Conkling, and pass the crown to Hayes. If he had learned wisdom from the wise Van Buren, he might have succeeded Grant as the New York leader succeeded Jackson.

BLAINE'S WASHINGTON HOUSE.

LIFE AND PUBLIC SERVICE

OF

JAMES G. BLAINE.

CHAPTER I.

FAMILY HISTORY AND BIRTH.

In casting one's nativity, the astrologer used celestial signs. The position of the heavens, the place of the sun, planets and stars, the combinations of occult influences at the time of a mortal birth, were supposed to effect character and life, and after the astrologer cast his horoscope he foretold, with a confidence which became his art, the kind of a man the swaddling clothes contained and the fate in store for him.

While the signs of the Zodiac and other celestial phenomena are not now supposed to influence character, we still consult nature's signs, if not to foretell, at least to account for human characteristics. Every student of anthropology admits that a Scotchman would be impossible in the Netherlands, or a Switzer in the flats of Italy. Family, too, or in other words, lineage, is deemed a momentous factor in shaping characteristics. One student says that in order to evolve the ideal man you must begin four hundred years before his birth. Another says if the virtues of his great-grandfathers are lacking in a man, it is pretty hard for him to stand up against their vices.

These thoughts naturally lead to mention of that environment amid which James G. Blaine made his earthly appearance. The estates of both lines of parents were located in Washington County, Pennsylvania. This is one of the South-western Counties of the State, abutting on West Virginia, and having for its eastern boundary the rugged lines of the Monongahela River. Its landscape is varied and beautiful, embracing high hills, picturesque valleys, and sparkling streams. Some of its hills reach the proportions of mountains. Krepps Knob, which rises from the valley and river at West Brownsville, overlooks an extended and variegated landscape, whose features are rich agricultural areas, slopes of stalwart forest, swift, meandering streams, and bluffy ridges which guard the rushing waters. Amid the plats of farm land, dotted with the homes of husbandmen, are cosy hamlets, with here and there populous towns whose glittering spires and roofs suggest their ambition to rank as cities. Down between the strong lines of hills which mark the course of the Monongahela are sequestered many busy centres, like Brownsville and Bridgeport, each the rival of the other as a manufacturing or commercial mart. Off to the extreme west, where the vista of hill, valley, wood, stream and farm stretches, begins to lose itself in the horizon's haze are seen the checkered outlines of West Virginia and Ohio, while far eastward the dark blue cloud which terminates the view and lends a background to the intermediate scene tells of the mighty barriers reared by the Alleghanies. From this superb "Crown of the Monongahela" one may see also what man has done to assist nature in redeeming a naturally fertile soil. The farms are large and well tended. Flocks and herds teem in the fenced enclosures or wander contentedly on the grassy hill sides. They are of the best breeds, and the value of their products evince the care bestowed upon their selection and propagation.

On a narrow strip of valley between the Monongahela River and the foot hills of Krepp's Knob stands the unpretentious town of. West Brownsville. It is irregularly built of brick and wood, and its topography is marred by ravines and, in later years, by railroad embankments. It has the air of business and thrift, and here and there are dwellings which tell of wealth and comfort. Their substantial build, antique architecture, and somewhat quaint surroundings, show that prosperous and cultivated families have found a home therein for several generations. On the opposite side of the river, in Fayette County, are the towns of East Brownsville and Bridgeport, two towns in one, and the real business centre of the valley, at this point. A bridge connects them with West Brownsville, so that there is a blending of populations and business, not to say a homogeniety of interests, which make practically an unincorporated city out of the three towns.

East Brownsville, or Brownsville proper, is even more medieval in appearance than its namesake on the west side of the river. Indeed, a visitor can hardly escape the impression that he is in some European town, whose front is the Rhine-like river, whose streets lead steeply up to castles on the overlooking heights, whose small old-fashioned houses, close upon the side walks, suggest the architecture of Scotland or Ireland. The cobble stone pavements, irregularly flagged sidewalks, medieval churches, and bluffs crowned with a few castellated mansions, complete the impression that here, as hardly elsewhere in the State, have been preserved the architectural ideals of those who cherished fond memories of their fatherlands.

The town is a busy, wealthy mart. The people are more than ordinarily intelligent. The many substantial mansions, the shade of old time breeding, the simplicity of dress and manners, the ease and comfort of inter communication, bespeak for the population a solidity that, with all its flavor of antiquity, highly recommends it to the nervously organized and energetic present.

Washington County, and for that matter entire Western Pennsylvania as comprised in the Allegheny, Monongahela and Ohio river sections, became historic ground at a very early period. It was the scene of explorations, forays and pitched battles at a time when English and French, with their respective Indian allies, were contending for this gateway to the Mississippi valley. At the same time pioneers from the East were forcing their way into the disputed sections, as settlers, traders or adventurers. Schooled to hardship, bold in project, skilled in border warfare, these became the worthy sires of those who afterwards shared with Washington the perils and fatigues of the American Revolution.

White men penetrated to the Monongahela as early as 1670, and shortly after La Salle made his celebrated tour of observation in the interest of the French government which ascertained the geographic and strategic importance of the "Forks of the Ohio." But it was not until 1753 that France deemed it necessary to send an army to protect her title against the aggressions of the English. The French marched from Lake Erie and began to fortify the line of the Ohio. England instructed Governor Dinwiddie, of Virginia, to fit out an expedition to meet and disperse the French invaders. The Governor sent George Washington, as a messenger, to command the French to evacuate their forts. His commission read :—" To George Washington, Esquire, one of the Adjutants General of the

The town is a busy, wealthy mart. The people are more than ordinarily intelligent. The many substantial mansions, the shade of old time breeding, the simplicity of dress and manners, the ease and comfort of inter communication, bespeak for the population a solidity that, with all its flavor of antiquity, highly recommends it to the nervously organized and energetic present.

Washington County, and for that matter entire Western Pennsylvania as comprised in the Allegheny, Monongahela and Ohio river sections, became historic ground at a very early period. It was the scene of explorations, forays and pitched battles at a time when English and French, with their respective Indian allies, were contending for this gateway to the Mississippi valley. At the same time pioneers from the East were forcing their way into the disputed sections, as settlers, traders or adventurers. Schooled to hardship, bold in project, skilled in border warfare, these became the worthy sires of those who afterwards shared with Washington the perils and fatigues of the American Revolution.

White men penetrated to the Monongahela as early as 1670, and shortly after La Salle made his celebrated tour of observation in the interest of the French government which ascertained the geographic and strategic importance of the "Forks of the Ohio." But it was not until 1753 that France deemed it necessary to send an army to protect her title against the aggressions of the English. The French marched from Lake Erie and began to fortify the line of the Ohio. England instructed Governor Dinwiddie, of Virginia, to fit out an expedition to meet and disperse the French invaders. The Governor sent George Washington, as a messenger, to command the French to evacuate their forts. His commission read:—"To George Washington, Esquire, one of the Adjutants General of the

BLAINE'S BIRTHPLACE.

troops and forces in the Colony of Virginia:—I, reposing especial trust and confidence in the ability, conduct and fidelity of you, the said George Washington, have appointed you my express messenger; and you are hereby authorized and empowered to proceed hence, with all convenient and possible despatch, to the part or place on the Ohio where the French have lately erected a fort, or forts, or where the commandant of the French forces resides, in order to deliver my letter and message to him; and after waiting, not exceeding one week for an answer, you are to take your leave and return immediately back.

"To this commission I have set my hand and caused the great seal of this dominion to be affixed at the city of Williamsburg, the seat of my government, this 30th day of October, in the twenty-seventh year of the reign of his majesty, George the Second, King of Great Britain &c., A. D., 1753. ROBERT DINWIDDIE.

The youthful Washington sped on his perilous journey, through deep forests, along Indian trails, and down the roaring stretches of the Monongahela. In a very short while he was to contribute to the making of a history which embraced Western Pennsylvania, and was written in blood. The campaigns of Braddock against the French were not models of generalship. They resulted in disasters, the chief of which was the bloody "Braddock's Field," now a famous pic-nic resort, where the visitor loves to recall the genius of the young Washington, to which the safety of the defeated and crest-fallen British regulars was due. These campaigns, and the Indian wars and massacres which attended or followed them, gave a glow to border history and became the source of countless traditions, which even the boys of to-day love to hear recounted. They introduced the daring borderer to the new and coveted territory, and these achieved what disciplined hosts had failed in. The War of the Revolution found Washington County, and a large part of the disputed territory, in the possession of hardy pioneers, mostly of Scotch-Irish origin, who had established flourishing trading posts and cleared farms. One of the most conspicuous of these posts was at Brownsville.

These men were true types of their race. Strong, courageous, adventure-loving, patriotic, they were in entire sympathy with the Revolution and active contributors to the cause of American Independence. Many enlisted in the Colonial armies, and one entire company dressed as Indians, marched the length of the State and joined Washington at Philadelphia. Their absence was taken advantage of by the unscrupulous enemy, who prepared the Indians for bloody raids and massacres, and filled the Western Counties with fear and grief. But for the undaunted character of the people the British policy of a "fire in the rear" of actual settlement might have proven dangerous to the success of the patriot cause.

While the events of the Revolution were breeding a sturdy citizenship in the Western Counties of the State, they were at the same time contributing to that independence of character which found outlet in revolt against the "Whiskey Tax" imposed by the Government. This tax was deemed unjust, and every attempt to collect it led to riot, arson, tar and feathers. At length, in 1794, open rebellion set in, which was only quelled by a national army. Pending these agitations, many momentous questions were discussed, especially those relating to the freedom of individuals and the rights of States, and not a few of the principles evolved bore fruit in the controversies relating to slavery and the great rebellion of 1861.

In the war of 1812, Washington County sent more than

her quota of volunteers, who swelled the army of General Harrison on the Lakes, and the garrisons at Baltimore and Washington. Their return enriched the history and traditions of the County, and stimulated the patriotism of the people. The County contributed a company for the defence of Texas in 1836, and sent many volunteers to the Mexican war in 1846. Thus inspired by a history and tradition which bristle with adventure, battles and patriotic efforts, the generations of Washington County as they passed away left to their successors a glorious example, and that high standard of patriotism which fitted them for the mighty struggle of 1861, and helped them to furnish to the nation so many evidences of devotion to country and to free institutions.

Among the adherents of the Scottish Prince Charlie, at the fatal battle of Culloden, was a soldier named Blaine. The name is that of a Highlander, whose clan may have had a seat near Loch Lomond. This indication of an ancient ancestry and a Scottish origin may gratify the curious, but it can scarcely add to the lustre of the man who has so distinguished the name in American annals. We know the drift of Scottish families, and even clans, to the north of Ireland, and their uses for purposes of conquest as well as their tenacious grasp of the soil. We know also of those Scotch-Irish qualities which became desirable in America, especially where they supplemented the efforts of the peace-loving Quakers. Both Quaker and German found the natural pioneers of North Ireland a splendid bulwark against Indian encroachment, and excellent levelers of primeval forest. They proved to be frontier men for the throng of non-combatants who made haste to profit by their energy and prowess. The broad expanse of soil, the opportunity for adventure, the continuous invitation to something new and better, seemed to beget in the Scotch Irishman an indifference to acres, and inspire a restlessness which caused him to vacate his conquests without a qualm, for the sake of others in advance of him.

Among those who followed early the fortunes of Penn, and who became the most useful of his pioneers in Pennsylvania, was one James Blaine. We find him a settler in the Cumberland Valley, near the town of Carlisle, as early as 1722-3, a member of the first Presbyterian church west of the Susquehanna, and a participant in the building of the old stone structure which still stands on the public square in Carlisle. It was here that his son, Ephraim Blaine, was born in the year 1740.

Ephraim Blaine was destined to lift the Blaine name into historic prominence, by his energetic and patriotic career as a soldier in the Revolutionary war. Among the first to join the patriot forces, he contributed his strength and fortune to the cause of independence. For three years his place was in the ranks, where, as colonel, he attracted the attention of Washington, who personally solicited his promotion to the position of Commissary General of Purchases. This promotion came at the age of thirty-eight, and that it was deserved was quickly shown by his courage, ability and self-sacrificial spirit. Through himself and the influence he exercised with friends, he was able at various times, when the Continental Treasury was depleted, to advance large sums of money for the purchase of arms, food and clothing, and during the trying winter at Valley Forge, Washington attributed the preservation of his army from starvation to the heroic efforts of his Commissary General. The General in Chief held him in the highest esteem, and their intercourse, as shown by letters official and unofficial, was almost brotherly. It is still one of the traditions of Carlisle that when Washington and his staff were on their way to suppress the Whiskey Rebellion they became the guests of Colonel Blaine, and while there learned of the dispersion of the insurgents. It is inferable from Colonel Blaine's liberality that he was possessed of considerable wealth, which seems to have been fortunately augmented by that of his wife, who was of the family of Galbraiths. He died at Carlisle in 1804, after serving a term as Sheriff of Cumberland County.

The domestic life of Col. Blaine was as interesting as his public career was patriotic. On the death of his first wife, he remained a widower for five years. Near his estate of "Middlesex" resided Judge Duncan, a man of social rank and high spirit. On account of a personal difficulty between the Judge and a lawyer of the Cumberland County Bar by the name of Lamberton, a challenge to fight a duel passed. The Judge chose James Blaine, Col. Blaine's son, as his second. The issue of the duel was the death of Judge Duncan by a rifle ball in the forehead. In due time Col. Blaine married Judge Duncan's widow. She survived him many years, and died in 1850, at the age of ninety years, at her mansion on Walnut street, Philadelphia, where she had lived for a long time in affluence and amid social distinction. The descendants and connections of Col. Blaine are numerous in Pennsylvania, and other parts of the Union. They number, among others, the Lyons, Russels, Ewings, Alexanders, Reeds, Walkers and Gillespies. The son of Col. Blaine's second wife, Dr. Stephen Duncan, became one of the wealthiest planters and most philanthropic man in the State of Mississippi.

His eldest son was James Blaine. He was given the benefit of an education at home and abroad and, having inherited ample means, he was diverted from the legal profession, for which he was designed by his parents, to that of diplomacy, in which he proved of service to the national government during his sojourn in Europe. He returned home in 1793, bringing with him, as a special bearer of dispatches, an important foreign treaty—the Jay Treaty. On his return he made Carlisle his home for a time, living the life of a well to do private gentleman. After the death of his father, and in possession of an increased fortune, he was attracted to Western Pennsylvania, as a field for investment and trade. He selected Brownsville as a likely site for his purposes and, upon his removal there, made some important investments and was selected as a justice of the peace. He was known as James Blaine, senior, and was a man of commanding appearance, being broad shouldered and fully six feet in height. His manners were pleasing and he was counted a great favorite among old and young. He was blessed with a family of four sprightly sons, Ephraim L., James, Samuel and William, born to him while in Carlisle, and for the most part educated there, prior to the general family removal to the West in 1818.

Besides the large tracts of land to which James Blaine, senior, acquired titles in and near West Brownsville, he owned the celebrated tract in Sewickly Township, Allegheny County, which is now in the possession of the Economite community. As he grew old and the importance of closer care to his estates increased, they were placed in charge of his eldest son Ephriam L. Blaine, who became a permanent resident of West Brownsville in 1818, and the manager of properties which, had they remained intact to this day, would have been worth millions. In 1825 he sold to the Economites, for $25,000, the tract which at present is valued at a princely sum.

Ephraim L. Blaine was born Feb, 28, 1796 and was well qualified mentally for his trust. He had supplemented a home education by travel in Europe, South America and the West Indies, and had brought to the West a fine physique and superior manners. For the time and place he was accounted rather aristocratic, and those censoriously inclined saw in him a man whose inclinations ran rather to pleasure than work. He entertained in a princely fashion and extended charity with lavish hand. From a strict dollar and cent point of view he was not a successful manager, and the vast estates under his control failed to realize as had been hoped for by his father and himself. In fact, they began to dwindle to such an extent as to cause their now owner to look about for some means of adding to an annual income.

But ere this happened, and while still a young man of twenty-four, tall and handsome, with eyes noted for their strength and brilliancy, fond of society, bearing a diploma from Washington College, flushed with pride and manly importance, he met the daughter of one of the leading families of Western Pennsylvania, Miss Maria Gillespie, and surrendered to her charms of mind and appearance. Her grandfather, Neal Gillespie, immigrated from the North of Ireland to Fayette County in 1771, where he at once assumed importance as a land holder and public spirited citizen. Though of Scotch-Irish origin, the family were ardent Catholics, and possessed of a character which developed strength under strain of circumstances. Neal Gillespie soon pushed his way westward of the Monongahela, and erected the first stone house beyond the stream, upon Indian Hill farm, in Washington County, Pa. This was in the year 1778. This house still stands, and in early times it was noted as the hospitable mansion of the Gillespie farm, where were wont to assemble the many handsome men and women of the section who loved the Gillespie name or were attracted by their hospitality.

This farm is now partly the site of West Brownsville, and included Krepps Knob. It was originally preempted by an old Indian named Indian Peter, and the deed to the estate was given by old Peter's widow and son. It reads as follows:—

March ye 3d 1784.

Memerandom of a Bargain mead between Marey Peters and William, oldest son, and Neal Gillespie, the agreement is thos that we the above do bargain and seal to sead Gillespie the Tract of land which we now poses and all the tenements and boundaries of said land at forty five Shillings per Aker, the tearm of Peaments the 15 of October next fower hundred pounds to be Paid in money or moneys worth for this Peament two ton of Iron at teen pence Pr pound and one negro at Preasement of two men, one hundred pounds more to be paid at the time of this Preasement, or Else to draw the trust for one year, the Remainder of the Purches money to be paid in two Peaments first in the year 1786, the next in the year 1788, each on October 15th, the above Marey Peters and william Peters asserts to meak the said Neal Gillespee a proper right for saidland for which we have set our hands and seals.

her
John McCortney. Marey xii Petters
mark
his
John Nixon. William xix Petters
mark

This fine estate descended to Neal Gillespie Jr. in 1800, and the rest of the Gillespie family scattered to various parts of the country to become the progenitors of a patriotic race of statesmen, scholars and citizens.

Maria Gillespie was the daughter of Neal Gillespie Jr. At the time she became engaged to Ephraim Lyon Blaine, she was counted as an heiress. Her beauty passed as a proverb, and it is not yet out of date in Western Pennsylvania. She was a woman of deep piety, a modest, re-

Burial-place of Blaine's Parents.

tiring Christian, sincere in conviction, yet not so wedded to creed as to refuse a lover of opposite belief, and somewhat given to the ways of the world.

The happy couple were married, presumably at the Gillespie mansion, as such would have been in accord with the custom of the days, and there they made their home for a time. Here were born their first son, and daughter. But the husband soon determined to set up for himself and to live in a style more becoming to his tastes. As the Gillespie estate had become largely his own, partly through his wife and partly by purchase, he selected as his future home the house in which his wife's grandfather had formerly resided, and by means of improvements converted it into a convenient and ostentatious residence. Thither they moved in the year 1829, and the mansion was dedicated by an evening party. Here Ephraim indulged to his heart's content his taste for visitation and travel and his love for a fine team and open-handed hospitality. He became noted for his dexterous horsemanship and his fine span of chestnut sorrels—Bolivar and Beaver—for his fashionable apparel, old-fashioned dinners, and elegant evening parties. In all this there was no economy, and but for the fact that his wife proved to be the more prudent manager, their estates must have suffered sooner than they really did.

It was while they resided in their new two-storied mansion, on the banks of the Monongahela, that their second son, and third child, James Gillespie Blaine, was born, January 31st, 1830. The event was heralded as such events are in a country town. It contributed joy to parents. It augured nothing of that fame which the child would, in manhood, attain. A family had been augmented by one. The future would make that one a host, contributing alike to family honor, to personal dis-

tiring Christian, sincere in conviction, yet not so wedded to creed as to refuse a lover of opposite belief, and somewhat given to the ways of the world.

The happy couple were married, presumably at the Gillespie mansion, as such would have been in accord with the custom of the days, and there they made their home for a time. Here were born their first son and daughter. But the husband soon determined to set up for himself and to live in a style more becoming to his tastes. As the Gillespie estate had become largely his own, partly through his wife and partly by purchase, he selected as his future home the house in which his wife's grandfather had formerly resided, and by means of improvements converted it into a convenient and ostentatious residence. Thither they moved in the year 1829, and the mansion was dedicated by an evening party. Here Ephraim indulged to his heart's content his taste for visitation and travel, and his love for a fine team and open-handed hospitality. He became noted for his dexterous horsemanship and his fine span of chestnut sorrels —Bolivar and Beaver—,for his fashionable apparel, old-fashioned dinners, and elegant evening parties. In all this there was no economy, and but for the fact that his wife proved to be the more prudent manager, their estates must have suffered sooner than they really did.

It was while they resided in their new two-storied mansion, on the banks of the Monongahela, that their second son, and third child, James Gillespie Blaine, was born, January 31st, 1830. The event was heralded as such events are in a country town. It contributed joy to parents. It augured nothing of that fame which the child would, in manhood, attain. A family had been augmented by one. The future would make that one a host, contributing alike to family honor, to personal dis-

CHAPTER II.

BOYHOOOD AND EDUCATION.

JAMES G. BLAINE'S boyhood was spent as that of other children, amid the influences of home, and subject to just those events which make up the history of early youth. Fortunately for him, his paternity contributed to good cheer, to freedom of action, to originality, to independence, while his maternity smoothed the harsher lines of character with the administrations of pious refinement. Home was for him a safeguard and assurance. Its restraints and encouragements were such as to balance, and the character formed therein might well prove to be natural and healthy. Fortunately also for him his environment was such as to conduce to fine physical growth. He could recreate at will on the paternal acres, and drink in life from the hill tops.

As his traits developed, he was found to be of sprightly, mischievous turn, given to physical motion and to boyhood pranks. Having access to the river, and a frequent witness of the boats that passed, he essayed a boat and navigable water of his own. He dammed up the stream that flowed down from Indian Hill and launched upon it a tiny bark of his own construction. But the neighboring boys repeatedly tore down his dam, and spoiled his navigation. He applied to the stalwart ferryman for help, and offered to bring his cows for an entire week if he would build him a dam out of stones so large that the mischievous boys could not move them. The ferryman accepted the offer, and little Jimmie soon had the satisfaction of a complete triumph over his enemies, for the rocks which the strong ferryman piled in resisted all the efforts of the boys for removal. His activity led him often to climb the height of Krepp's Knob, whence he delighted in the scenery, to count the river boats and to indulge his childish imagination. "There," said he to a companion, as he pointed to the Virginia outlines, "is the end of the world, and I am going there some day." As he grew in years and confidence, he delighted in hunting. Maternal anxiety forbade him the use of a gun, so that he was forced to depend upon axe and dog as a means of capturing the rabbit by day and the coon by night.

During Blaine's boyhood the public school was not a satisfactory institution, if it existed at all in Brownsville. His mother, being a woman of superior culture, preferred to instruct her own children. For some time she taught them in the school of her model home, but was forced to desist through increasing cares. An old schoolmate of hers, Mrs. Matilda Dorsey, opened a subscription school near by and James was entered as a pupil. He was eight years old and, as his teacher says, a ruddy cheeked lad, full of frolic and harmless mischief. Though young, he was a leader among the boys. He learned his lessons with little effort, and had plenty of time to invent plans and amuse himself at the expense of others. It was summer and blackberries were ripe. There was a great patch near the school-house. *Jim*, as Mrs. Dorsey called him, used to revel among the fruit, and, after he had filled himself, would gather a supply with which to prank it in the school. The dozing scholars became objects of his aim, and they were awakened by a well directed berry from Jim's bountiful supply, much to the amusement of the entire school. The teacher reprimanded Jim, forbade him to enter the patch, and tried to frighten him by telling him it was full of copperhead snakes. She utterly failed in her object, for the next day Jim came loaded for a fresh bombardment. It was a hot day and the teacher herself fell asleep. Jim took aim and landed a blackberry on the point of her nose. She awakened suddenly and irately. Instinct told her whence the missile had come and she summoned the culprit before her.

"Did you shoot that berry?" she demanded angrily.

No response came, but Jim's downcast features suddenly lighted up with a smile.

"Did you shoot that berry?" she again fiercely demanded.

"No'm," replied Jim; "I shot *you*."

Mrs. Dorsey would fain have laughed outright, but fearing a loss of dignity and influence in the school, she drew the offender across her lap and administered proper punishment with a book. She declared that Jim did not squirm under the blows and gave her no sort of satisfaction by opening a childish yell. The same good lady, continuing her reminisences, says the boys used to plague Jim by calling him "nosy," which was very naughty in them, though not inappropriate owing to the prominence of that organ. He got a sweet revenge though, for he was always at the head of his class, always knew his lessons, and delighted in hard tasks, especially in spelling.

While pranky and even boisterous in school, he was rather shy and reticent in society. The storekeeper once played a practical joke on him by wrapping up an article he had not asked for. He returned with it to the store, to be greeted with roars of laughter by the loungers. Shortly after, the storekeeper was measuring grain and keeping tally by laying a cob on the ledge for each bushel measured. Jim looked demurely on till the measuring was finished, when he quietly knocked the cobs off, thus compelling a second measurement.

He was the most tender hearted of boys. Any tale of suffering awakened his sympathies and he would go to any extent to relieve it. A poor widow, with several children to support, was compelled to sell her cow to the butcher. Blaine happened along and found the widow crying. On learning her story, he started after the butcher, and offered all he had on his person, even to a watch presented to him by his uncle, to redeem the cow. The butcher remained unmoved, whereupon young Blaine burst into tears, and for weeks talked frequently of the poor widow, and the misfortune he had tried in vain to relieve.

It is easy to see that a boy of the precocity of young Blaine would soon outgrow the opportunities for schooling which Brownsville afforded. A change would have to come, and it soon did come, but not of his own volition. During his early childhood, his father became interested in a strong bridge over the Monongahela a short distance above his home. He regarded the project as one sure to enhance the value of his property, and subscribed largely to the stock. The bridge was finished in 1833. Stores and boat-yards were opened in West Brownsville. Lots increased in value. Ephraim Blaine was soon counted as a rich and fortunate man. He indulged his extravagant tastes more largely than ever. But soon a violent reaction set it. Property fell to ruinous prices. Disaster followed disaster, and soon the enterprising financier found himself in straightened circumstances. Fortunately his great natural gifts, his culture, his manners and charities, had brought him social and political influence, and though Washington County was decidedly Democratic, he conducted a successful campaign in 1842 as Whig candidate for the office of Prothonotary and was elected. In order to fulfil the duties of the office Ephraim Blaine moved to Washington, the County seat, in the latter part of 1842 or early part of 1843. He had resolved to give his son James a collegiate education at the college there, and that he might prepare for it, he was sent to Lancaster, Ohio, where in the home of Hon. Thomas Ewing, then Secretary of the Treasury, he enjoyed along with Thomas Ewing, Junior, the tutorship of William Lyons, brother of Lord Lyons, and uncle of the then British Minister at Washington. The cultured family of Mr. Ewing, an uncle of Blaine, exerted an excellent influence on the young student, and under a tutorship of one chosen to care for an own child, he soon completed his preparatory course. In the fall of 1843 he was ready to enter college, and returned home for that purpose.

The institution which was to receive him was the Washington and Jefferson College. It had its origin, as the colleges of New England had, in the general respect for religion and learning, and the need of institutions which might be not only conservers of these things and centres for instruction in them, but sources of supply to the ministry. Before they had made a home for themselves the people of Western Pennsylvania made a home for those things of the spirit which were dearest to them. It is a rare devotion which inspires the building of churches and schools in advance of full provision for more material needs. It belongs only to the sturdiest class of men—men who have done much for the world; and is worth noting where we find it.

It was mainly with the purpose of providing a means for the nurture of a ministry at home that the Rev. John M'Millan, Rev. Joseph Smith, and Rev. Thomas Dodd established schools of their own at Chartiers, Buffalo, and

Ten Mile, in Washington County, about 1780. The most successful of these Latin schools, as they were called, was that under the charge of the Rev. John M'Millan, and when an academy was established at Canonsburgh, in 1791, his prosperous school was merged in it. One of the principals of this academy, James Carnahan, was afterward President of Princeton, and one of his successors became the first president of the college which grew out of it, and which in 1802 was chartered by the State and named Jefferson. It is not a thing of which Jefferson boasts, but it was the first institution of the higher learning west of the Alleghanies.

In the same county another college had grown up by the side of Jefferson, called Washington. It was also sprung from an academy, and in that form was only five years younger than the town of Washington in which it stood, having been chartered in 1787. The names of the three ministers who in a remote way founded Jefferson stand first on the list of the incorporators of Washington Academy. In 1805 Rev. Matthew Brown became at the same time the first pastor of the Presbyterian Church at Washington, and Principal of the Academy, and under him it met such success that in 1806 the State Legislature gave the trustees a college charter. It had scarcely been established when a union was proposed with its young neighbor Jefferson, but this wise move was not fully accomplished until 1869. By the act which united the two colleges the alumni of both are accounted as alumni of the new College of Washington and Jefferson, and Mr. Blaine's college may therefore be said to be Washington and Jefferson, though in fact it was Washington.

This was probably, when James Blaine entered it in 1843, as good a small college as he would have found by going farther from home; and it had the advantage of all the lesser colleges; the close relation of pupil and teacher. The class with which young Blaine entered was of about the usual number—thirty-three.

One of his classmates, Alexander M. Gow, of Fontanelle, Iowa, writes of Mr. Blaine's youth, that while at College he was "a boy of pleasing manners and agreeable address, quite popular among the students and in society. He was a better scholar than student. Having very quick perceptions and a remarkable memory, he was able to catch and retain easily what came to others by hard work. In the literary society he was a politician, and it was there, I think, that he received a good deal of the training that made him what he is." The mother of his college room-mate remembers very well when her son brought him home to spend a vacation. She speaks of him as a "raw, angular fellow, with a big nose," and says that when she met him a year or two ago she was "astounded to find that he remembered every incident of those boyish days, and could tell her many things which she had forgotten. He remembered all the family, their relatives and the neighbors, and could talk of his visit as though it had been but yesterday."

H. H. M. Pusey, of Iowa, another of his classmates, and a member of Congress from Iowa, says:

"James Blaine, as I remember him, was a pretty well-built boy and a hard student. He had an impediment of his speech, however, which prevented him from joining in our debates and declamations, but he could distance all his classmates in the matter of studies, and his memory was remarkable. We had in the college a literary society, of which I was president about the time Blaine was sixteen years old. One day he came to me and said: 'B-b ill, I would like to be p-president of the literary. Can you

WASHINGTON AND JEFFERSON COLLEGE.

f-f-fix it for me?' I answered: 'Why what do you know about the literary society? You have never taken any part in the debates and have always preferred to pay your fine to taking active part. Do you know anything about parliamentary practice?' He replied: 'No, but I can c-c-commit Cushing's Manual to memory in one night.' Well, the result was that at the next meeting I 'fixed it' for him, and at the meeting the next week Blaine was elected president, vice Pusey, term expired. As he had promised, he committed the entire contents of Cushing's Manual, and he proved the best president the literary society of the college ever had.

"I remember one day his father told him to get up early and go to the market to buy a turkey. He gave him a dollar, which was a good deal of money in those days. Well, James brought home the bird and handed it to old Dinah, the colored cook of the Blaine family. When the elder Blaine came down to breakfast Dinah greeted him: 'Mars Blaine, dat dar turkey what Mars Jim buyed dis mawin' am de quarest turkey I's ever seed. Deed it is, Mars Blaine.'

"'Why, what's the matter with it, Dinah? ain't it big enough?' replied the old gentleman. 'It ought to be, surely; Jim paid a dollar for it.'

"'Oh yes, Mars Blaine, de turkey is big 'nuff, but it am de funniest turkey dis yer nigger ever seed.'

"'Mars Blaine' went out to the kitchen to look at the 'turkey' and found it to be a ten-year-old goose.

"He called Jim down and hauled him over the coals, saying: 'Why, Jim, you ought to be ashamed of yourself. Fifteen years old and can't tell a turkey from a goose!'

"Jim hung his head and simply replied: 'Why, how's

a boy to tell a turkey from a goose when its feathers are off.'"

Another who seems to have known him says:

"To the new scholars who entered in succeeding classes he was a hero—uniformly kind to them, ready to give assistance and advice, and eager to make pleasant their path in college life. His handsome person and neat attire; his ready sympathy and prompt assistance; his frank, generous nature, and his brave manly bearing, made him the best known, the best loved, and the most popular boy at college. He was the arbiter among younger boys in all their disputes, and the authority with those of his own age on all questions."

Young Blaine's chief diversion while in college seems to have been the hunting of the bushy-tailed fox, which abounded in the region. In his sportsman's excursions he often accompanied a negro named Randolph Tearle, who was accounted the most skilful huntsman in the valley. Washington County is in the midst of gently undulating hills, covered with generous forests, and was a fruitful field for this kind of sport when James Blaine roamed over it as a boy. The county is now, as it had begun to be then, a rich agricultural region. More wool is taken from the sheep that pasture on its hills than from those of any other county in the United States, and it has fairly productive beds of coal. On its streams the college lad beguiled his idle hours boating or fishing. The Monongahela River is the eastern boundary of Washington County, and there are numerous creeks within its limits. One of his acquaintances in the town of Washington says; "There is not a stump or rock on these hills that

Blaine doesn't know. He knows the country about here better than most of the people who have never lived anywhere else. He must have scoured these hills while he was a boy.

"He is very well remembered by every one about his old home, of course—that is the privilege of all men who go away from any home to become famous. But not all men in whose careers their ancient neighbors find cause for honest pride, are held in such kindly remembrance. In Brownsville and Washington the visitor's ear is assailed with reminiscences of his early years. These are not all memorable or even very entertaining, but they are invariably delivered with a heartiness which gives them a value as expressions of the popular liking for Mr. Blaine among those who have known him intimately. Perhaps he is liked not only because these people remember him pleasantly, but because he remembers them pleasantly, for when he has returned to his old home his capacious memory has accompanied him, and his success has not taught him to deny the humblest of his old associates.

"The class list will have shown his standing upon graduation,—certainly not discreditable to one who is remembered as a good but not sedulous student by his companions. It is said that he excelled in mathematics and the languages. It was a fit close to his college career, as well as a pathetic beginning of his life-work, that his commencement oration should have been upon "The Duty of an Educated American."

An able biographer, in describing the college career of James G. Blaine, and writing in the year 1884, says:—

"To the new-comers and the freshmen, Jim Blaine was always a hero. To them he was uniformly kind; ever ready to assist and advise them, and to make smooth and pleasant their initiation into college life. His handsome person; his ready sympathy and prompt assistance; his frank and generous nature, and his brave, manly bearing, made him the best known, the best loved, and the most popular boy at college. He was the arbiter among younger boys in all their disputes, and the authority with those of his own age on all questions.

"He was a natural student, excelling pre-eminently in mathematics and English branches, showing also good work in the dead languages of the classics. Mathematics without question were to him a pleasure. He threw into the pursuit of them all the ardor of a budding enthusiasm. He delighted in the close reasoning; the subtle logic; the inevitable and invincible proofs of which the problems and positions were susceptible. He enjoyed a sort of personal satisfaction in the triumph of a mathematical principle, as though he, its demonstrator, was also its inventor. He was always perfect in mathematical recitations, and was the idol of his teacher, Professor Aldrich. Possessed of an extraordinary memory and great quickness of apprehension, he was able to take strong hold of the subjects he studied and retain them.

"One peculiar trait of his character as then formed, and which he constantly exhibited, was perfect self-reliance. While others might follow the ordinary beaten tracks, he took delight in getting out of them. Notably so when one warm sunny afternoon in May, 1846, at a recitation in mathematics, he stood before his class, and having drawn the figure on the blackboard, he was proceeding to prove the proposition it contained when he was interrupted by the professor.

"James, you are not following the mode of proof of the author."

To which the lad, with quick, earnest tones, replied:

"What does it matter if I can demonstrate the principle

of the proposition in some other way than he has done?"

"The boys laughed; Professor Aldrich had no answer for the bold innovator, who, amid deep awakened interest, continued his demonstration and proved the proposition and his right to a new demonstration. Such originality of thought and ability to lead, as showing that he was able to reach a result by his own ingenuity, and by some other than the beaten way, that marked this occasion, is the same characteristic that so often since has amazed and captured the great audience of the United States—his fellow-citizens.

"Jim Blaine possessed the faculty of always making a good showing in his classes, and even when not entirely prepared, his quickness and apparent familiarity with his lessons would carry him safely through. And when such an occasion did occur, it required shrewder professors than Washington College boasted of having to detect his deficiencies. This prominence in his class was conceded by his classmates to be due to his talents and industry, and occasioned, therefore, no jealousy nor hatred of him, a fact that can be the more easily appreciated when it is remembered that while Euclid presented no difficulties—not even the old bugbear *pons asinorum*—to Jim Blaine, Tacitus was equally a friend of the young student; he was thoroughly familiar with the Greek poets.

"Fond of literature for the delightful insight it gave him into the companionship of great minds, and the deep vista of other worlds than were visible from Brownsville, he readily devoured such books as the college library afforded, and the rooms of the various societies contained. This was a matter of delight to the rapidly expanding mind of the boy, and the highways and by-ways of Shakespeare, the fine philosophy of Bacon, the rare pages of Ben Johnson, the lighter fancies of Oliver Goldsmith mingled their varied influences with the greater histories and the more modest story of the young Republic. To the tale of 1776 and the early days of his country's career young Blaine lent more than a willing ear, and was never tired of the story of how large a part his great grandfather had played in that sad yet glorious drama. The taste for history, too, founded a solid taste in literature that has ever since continued to such excellent advantage, and notably makes brilliant the pages of "Twenty Years of Congress."

"Washington College, like similar institutions, sustained two literary societies, the "Washington" and the "Union," which were the pride of the college. There was between them always a keen and honorable rivalry. The canvass for new members at the opening of each term of college was very lively. New students were buttonholed on every street corner, at every boarding-house, or "fort," as it was termed, by some one of the ardent Unionists or Washingtonians. Jim Blaine was an ardent and energetic adherent of the "Washington," and made an admirable canvasser for recruits. He was always alert, and succeeded in winning many converts. It was here that he first displayed his remarkable aptitude as a presiding officer, and he displayed it in a way thoroughly characteristic. Having been elected archon, or president, he committed Cushing's Manual to memory before his installation, and calmly astonished his most intimate friends by the perfect ease and promptness with which he made his decisions and their absolute correctness. His membership in Washington demonstrated that he was a natural debater, not a wrangler, but a reasoning disputant, who delighted in convincing his opponent, if possible, that he was wrong. Political subjects in those days were his chief delights, and his arguments with one or two staunch Democrats among the students are not yet forgotten by his classmates.

"At this period young Blaine was tall and well developed for a boy of his years. He was never fond of the rough games played by the students, football being apparently one of his aversions; yet, when he occasionally could be induced to take part in the game, he would acquit himself as well with his feet as he did elsewhere with his head. Indeed, in athletic sports he was less of a leader than in any other place, seeming to be willing to concede superiority to others in those accomplishments which could be of no benefit in future life beyond laying the foundation for a good physique, of which he seemed conscious he was even then fully possessed.

"His ambition to excel never slept, yet it never led him into doing anything which could possibly injure a fellow-student. The selfishness which is necessary to make one try to excel was not with him of the kind to work a wrong on another. He was never so much wrapped up in himself that he could not concede a full measure of praise to a successful classmate, and acknowledge his merits in a just and proper manner, and to this sense of justice was added a strong and never-swerving spirit of forgiveness.

"Such qualities naturally drew the boys to him. That personal magnetism which draws and binds friends to one's self was a marked feature in his character. While never a fop, he was always neat in his dress, never appearing in the street or in class in disordered attire. He was fond of young ladies' society, but never neglected his studies to indulge in that pleasure. The idea that young Blaine was bashful or timid in the company of young ladies was never correct, and in the happy days beside the Monongahela there was no boy in the town who could make himself more agreeable during the long, white winter evenings or in a ramble over the summer hills, clad in all the glorious verdure of the woods.

"And young Blaine's popularity among the young ladies of Washington was but the echo of his popularity everywhere. His obedience to the rules of the institution made him popular with the faculty, especially its president, the Rev. David McConaughy, D. D., the honored and faithful pastor of the Presbyterian Church at Washington, the church young Blaine attended every Sabbath morning.

"It can be said of him, as perhaps of few others that have passed through college, that he carefully guarded his habits, and left college, as he entered it, without any stain upon his name, and without having been guilty of those excesses that sometimes leave their imprint in after life because of habits formed that were hard to get rid of.

"It can be also truly said of him that he was, although surrounded by considerable temptation, strongly temperate, and that he rather prided himself upon the fact that he would not touch intoxicating liquor of any kind. In his intercourse with his classmates he was polite and gentlemanly; always maintaining a certain self-respect, he commanded admiration, was careful not to wound their feelings, and left them at the close of his college life without an enemy among the number. He graduated with honor to himself, and left behind him a reputation for integrity, good behavior, and scholarship which few students attain."

Mr. Blaine graduated on the 25th of September, 1847, at the age of seventeen years and eight months, with the full approval of the faculty of his college, which consisted of: Rev. David McConaughy, D. D., LL. D., presi-

MRS. JAMES G. BLAINE.

by hundreds, fitted by thorough collegiate training for every variety of profession and other respectable service. More than three thousand graduates, besides an almost equal number who have taken a partial course, embracing fourteen hundred ministers, seventeen hundred and fifty lawyers, four hundred physicians, six or eight United States senators, six cabinet officers, fifty or more representatives in congress, sixty judges, forty-five college presidents, seventy-five college professors, twenty-five professors in theological seminaries, as many principals of female seminaries; to say nothing of the headships of countless academies—surely this is a production of cultured men which may be safely put in competition with that of any other community in kind or value, or with any scale of material interests actual or possible in like circumstances. Proud therefore as we may be to be reckoned in the front rank of the world's competitors as producers of the world's finest wool, and rejoicing as we do in the heritage of a soil and climate unsurpassed for the multiplied and varied comforts of life, our highest exultation is in the educated men who have carried the name and fame of Washington County as a chief home of culture into the foremost rivalry of our country, and made it known across the seas."

In writing to the people of his native county on the occasion of their Centennial celebration in 1881, James G. Blaine pleasantly enlarged upon the same topic. "I had anticipated," he writes, "great pleasure in being present at the Centennial celebration of the erection of Washington County, but the national sorrow which shadows every household detains me here.

"I shall perhaps never again have the opportunity of seeing so many friends of my youth, and so many of my blood and kindred, and you may well conceive my disappointment is great.

"The strong attachment which I feel for my county, the pride which I cherish in its traditions, and the high estimate which I have always placed on the character of its people, increase with years and reflection. The pioneers were strong-hearted, God-fearing, resolute men, wholly, or almost wholly, of Scotch or Scotch-Irish descent. They were men who, according to an inherited maxim, never turned their backs on friend or enemy.

"For twenty years, dating from the middle period of the revolution, the settlers were composed very largely of men who had themselves served in the Continental army, many of them as officers, and they imparted an intense patriotism to the public sentiment.

"It may be among the illusions of memory, but I think I have nowhere else seen the Fourth of July and Washington's birthday celebrated with such zeal and interest as in the gatherings I there attended. I recall a great meeting of the people on the Fourth of July, 1840, on the border of the county, in Brownsville, at which a considerable part of the procession was composed of vehicles containing Revolutionary soldiers. I was but ten years old, and may possibly mistake, but I think there were more than two hundred of the grand old heroes. The modern cant and criticism which we sometimes hear about Washington not being, after all, a very great man, would have been dangerous talk on that day and in that assemblage.

"These pioneers placed a high value on education, and while they were still on the frontier, struggling with its privations, they established two excellent colleges, long since prosperously united in one. It would be impossible to overstate the beneficent and wide-spread influence which Washington and Jefferson colleges have exerted on the civilization of that great country which lies between the Alleghanies and the Mississippi River. Their graduates have been prominent in the pulpit, at the bar, on the bench and in the high stations of public life. During my service of eighteen years in Congress, I met a larger number of the Alumni of Washington and Jefferson than of any other single college in the Union.

"I make this statement from memory, but I feel assured that a close examination of the rolls of the two Houses, from 1863 to 1881, would fully establish its correctness. Not only were the two colleges founded and well sustained, but the entire educational system of the county, long before the school tax and public schools, was comprehensive and thorough. I remember that in my boyhood there were ten or eleven academies or select schools in the county, where lads could be fitted for college.

"In nearly every instance the Presbyterian pastor was the principal teacher. Many who will be present at your Centennial will recall the succession of well drilled students who came for so many years from the tuition of Dr. McCluskey, at West Alexander, from Rev. John Stockton, at Cross Creek, from Rev. John Eagleson, of Buffalo, and from others of like worth and education.

"It was inevitable that a county thus peopled should grow in strength, wisdom and wealth. Its sixty thousand inhabitants are favored far beyond the average lot of man. They are blessed with a fertile soil, and with the health-giving climate which belongs to the charmed latitude of the fortieth parallel, the middle of the wheat and corn belt of the continent. Beyond this they enjoy the happy and ennobling influences of scenery as grand and as beautiful as that which lures tourists thousands of miles beyond the sea. I have myself visited many of the celebrated spots in Europe and America, and I have nowhere witnessed a more attractive sight than was familiar to my boyhood from the old Indian Hill farm where I was born, and where my great-grandfather, the elder Neal Gillespie, settled before the outbreak of the Revolution.

"The majestic sweep of the Monongahela through the foot-hills of the Alleghanies, with the chain of mountains, but twenty miles distant, in full view, gave an impression of beauty and sublimity which can never be effaced.

"I talk thus familiarly of localities and of childhood incidents, because your assemblage, though composed of thousands, will, in effect, be a family reunion, where the only thing in order will be tradition, recollection and personal history. Identified, as I have been, for twenty-eight years, with a great and noble people in another section of the Union, I have never lost any of my attachment for my native county and native state. The two feelings no more conflict than does a man's love for his wife and his love for his mother. Wherever I may be in life, or whatever my fortune, the county of Washington, as it anciently was, taking all the state, south and west of the Monongahela, will be sacred to my memory. I shall always recall with pride that my ancestry and kindred were, and are, not inconspicuously connected with its history, and that on either side of the beautiful river, in Protestant and Catholic cemeteries, five generations of my own blood sleep in honored graves."

James entered college at the unusually early age of thirteen, yet he appears to have been thoroughly equipped for his undertaking, if not in that proficiency which books afford, at least in native powers sufficient for any emergency. A frequent lady visitor to the Blaine home says "that the young collegian was familiarly known as "Jim." All the members of the family were fond of society excepting him. His idea was a book and he would read anything he could get hands on. Though she knew him as "Jim," she paid many visits before she got sight of him. He was not a fine looking boy at that stage of his career. His development was just beginning. He had a large frame, but was thin and ungainly. His clothes sat awkwardly on him and he had no apparent pride in personal appearance. His books were a hobby, and his ungainly way that of the student. As he grew older he began to fill out and by the time he graduated he was a comely youth.

All the narratives of this portion of his life confirm the impression that he was shy of society, awkward in demeanor, and inclined to solitude. He was not an active participant in college sports. The literary and debating societies found in him a special supporter. He wrote an excellent essay and read before his class with clearness and vigor. In all respects he was diligent, persistent and frank, seeking rather the roots of things than the things themselves. Though easily the leading man of his class none prophesied for him so brilliant a career as he shaped in practical life. He seemed to be created for emergencies, and responded to a sudden call with remarkable aptitude. He was most original and powerful when he had least time to think, and when exigency stirred to effort. He would do in the midst of trial what another could not accomplish, and as he rose to the occasion it was easy to discern that more than ordinary genius reposed within him. His tastes were mathematical and logical rather than classical. In debate he was argumentative rather than persuasive, and he preferred political themes to those of a less lively type. He was a Whig by birthright and during his second collegiate year, in 1844, the brilliancy of his arguments respecting the Mexican war drew general remark. The Whigs had a log cabin headquarters near the college and there he often found outlet for his views among the leaders of the party. To those who witnessed his love of argument, versatility of talent and pertinacity of sentiment it was not strange that he developed into a politician. He was an ardent Henry Clay man, and study of the great Kentucky leader may have had much to do with his masterly oratory, his economic views and his parliamentary powers.

While in college he held the respect and confidence of his instructors. He boarded for a time with Professor Nicholas Murray, who held the chair of ancient languages, and between the two the warmest affection existed. When the Professor died, Blaine interested himself in raising a subscription toward a monument, and the substantial tribute to his memory which to-day ornaments the college campus is chiefly due to the exertions of his affectionate pupil.

Perhaps the most remarkable quality of the collegian was his memory. This he developed by rigid discipline, and it has proven one of the essential secrets of his success in life. While he read much, he arranged and digested so as to leave an indelible impression on his mind. Men, measures, dates, events, took classified shape with him, and he recalled each and all with phenomenal readiness.

He graduated in 1847, at the early age of seventeen. The honors of his class were divided between him and two other students. He stepped forth into the world with retiring inclinations, but a stern necessity forced him into combat. He could not hope for further assistance from his father, whose remaining property was fast slipping away, nor did there seem to be anything in his line about home which he could turn to speedy and practical account. The family must lose him, but that loss would prove the nation's gain. The discipline of self-strife for

CHAPTER III.

A TEACHER.

It was not long before an opportunity opened to the ambitious young man. Through the influence of Hon. Thomas Ewing, he was offered a position in the Western Military Academy, at Blue Lick Springs, Kentucky, of which Col. Thornton F. Johnson was principal. The place he assumed was the chair of mathematics. Into the profession of a teacher he entered with his whole nature, and was from the first a successful instructor. The same characteristics which led him to defend the smaller and weaker boys in college, made him a favorite with his pupils. He had a natural and strong repugnance to every kind of oppression. He would not stand quietly and see a strong boy abuse a weak one, or silently allow a burly boy to tease a timid one. One of his scholars writing from Kentucky in 1863, says:—"He should have been a judge. His keen sense of justice and his wonderful ability to discover deceit or sham made him a master of the situation. They often managed to deceive the other teachers, and could offer frail excuses to the principal, often with impunity, but to Mr. Blaine, never. He knew before we spoke, and often kindly saved the boys from lying by rebuking them first and letting them explain afterwards. I never knew of his making a mistake in that matter."

In the Military Institute there were between four and five hundred pupils, many of them of that fiery temperament incident to the locality and era. They were of diverse politics, and not a few of them became conspicuous in military and political life, dividing on the lines drawn by the great war of the Rebellion. When one of them, who became a prominent Tennessee lawyer, heard of Blaine's advocacy of the abolition doctrine, he said to a friend:—"He is consistent to his old life. It was natural for him to dislike slavery." In that institute Blaine was clearly a favorite. He knew every boy by name, and knew also their individual tastes and characters. He sympathized with the suffering and enjoyed the sports of the strong. As a teacher he was clear and simple in his explanations and deeply in earnest in imparting information. Yet not even his aptitude and earnestness as teacher could suppress his inclination for the legal profession, for which his native fearlessness and insight into human nature seemed to especially fit him.

Twenty miles away from Blue Lick Springs was Millersburg, in which was located a Young Ladies' Seminary, over which the wife of Col. Johnson presided. This institution contained the magnet which was to attract the young professor and influence his entire after life. She was Miss Harriet Stanwood of Augusta, Maine, a descendant of old Puritan stock in a direct line from the Stanwoods of Ipswich, Massachusetts. She resided with her sister in Millersburg, and was a teacher in the female seminary. Young Blaine became enamored of her talents and person and they became engaged. They were married in Pittsburg in 1851.

Of Blaine's career, while a Professor in the Blue Lick Springs Institute, the late John F. Edmonds of Hopkinsville, Ky., writes:—"I shall never forget his manly, generous friendship. I was involved in a difficulty with a boy belonging to a wealthy and influential family, and in the course of the quarrel he applied a vulgar epithet to

diverse politics, and not a few of them became conspicuous in military and political life, dividing on the lines drawn by the great war of the Rebellion. When one of them, who became a prominent Tennessee lawyer, heard of Blaine's advocacy of the abolition doctrine, he said to a friend:—"He is consistent to his old life. It was natural for him to dislike slavery." In that institute Blaine was clearly a favorite. He knew every boy by name, and knew also their individual tastes and characters. He sympathized with the suffering and enjoyed the sports of the strong. As a teacher he was clear and simple in his explanations and deeply in earnest in imparting information. Yet not even his aptitude and earnestness as teacher could suppress his inclination for the legal profession, for which his native fearlessness and insight into human nature seemed to especially fit him.

Twenty miles away from Blue Lick Springs was Millersburg, in which was located a Young Ladies' Seminary, over which the wife of Col. Johnson presided. This institution contained the magnet which was to attract the young professor and influence his entire after life. She was Miss Harriet Stanwood of Augusta, Maine, a descendant of old Puritan stock in a direct line from the Stanwoods of Ipswich, Massachusetts. She resided with her sister in Millersburg, and was a teacher in the female seminary. Young Blaine became enamored of her talents and person and they became engaged. They were married in Pittsburg in 1851.

Of Blaine's career, while a Professor in the Blue Lick Springs Institute, the late John F. Edmonds of Hopkinsville, Ky., writes:—"I shall never forget his manly, generous friendship. I was involved in a difficulty with a boy belonging to a wealthy and influential family, and in the course of the quarrel he applied a vulgar epithet to

Philadelphia Blind Asylum.

my mother for which I knocked him down. I was arraigned before the faculty, sharply reproved for violating the rules and threatened with disgrace if I did not make an ample apology. The faculty were all against me except Prof. Blaine. He arose and with much warmth and feeling said that he could not withhold his sympathy for a boy when love and reverence for his mother involved him in trouble. "This boy," said he, "only resented a foul insult to his absent mother. What boy of manliness and honor, especially with the peculiar training of a Kentucky boy, would not resent such an insult more quickly than an insult to himself? I will not only not consent to censure him, but say that I think he did right, and that I feel more like praising than reproving him." This brief, magnetic speech worked like magic on the strict minds of the faculty and the offender was turned loose with a gentle admonition.

Blaine's reputation for courage was established early in his career at Blue Lick. A bloody fight between the faculty of the school and the owners of the Springs, involving some question about the removal of the school, took place. During the affray young Blaine behaved in the bravest manner, fighting hard but keeping cool. Revolvers and knives were freely used by the combatants, but the Pennsylvania teacher used only his well-disciplined muscles. The faculty won, and the prestige of having been a leader in a winning fight, a giant in the fray, was not in the least detrimental to the success of the aspiring pedagogue.

Another incident of his Kentucky career that experted a striking influence upon his life was his contact with the evils of slavery. He met it face to face, he felt its influence, he knew its demoralizing power, and he saw everywhere around him the wreck of great principles which it had wrought. The effect of this contact upon Mr. Blaine in after years was very marked, and his position on the slavery question, even while in the homes of those fostering the system, was that of decided opposition to the iniquity in every form and shape.

In an editorial, printed in the *Kennebec Journal*, January 15th, 1855, Mr. Blaine thus throws a side light on his life in Kentucky and the unshaken opinions that he then formed concerning slavery:

The "Age" Growing Personal.

We find the following precious *morceau* in the *Age* of Saturady last:

"One of the editors of the new Morrill organ in this city has too recently partaken of the 'slaveholder's salt,' and reposed beneath the shadow of the 'peculiar institution,' to authorize him to lecture contemporaries on their duty to the cause of 'freedom.' We would recommend to his consideration Shakespeare's advice to new beginners in the art theatrical."

"We—the editor referred to in this *would-be* severe paragraph—have to plead guilty to a residence of four years, prior to and including 1850, in the State of Kentucky. We were engaged in what we still consider the honorable capacity of a teacher, in a literary institution, then and now in deservedly high standing with the several states, both North and South, which patronize and sustain it. Invited to take the position for a certain pecuniary consideration, which we regularly received, and having to the best of our ability and to the satisfaction of all concerned discharged our duties, we have been under the impression that the matter was closed and nothing due from either party to the other in the way of personal obligation or political fealty. The *Age*, however, seems to think that having partaken of the "slaveholder's salt" (for which we paid), we should be dumb to the slaveholder's wrong-doings. So conscious are they of the potency of a little "administration *salt*" in shutting their own mouths and stifling their real sentiments on the slavery question, that they cannot conceive of any one taking a more independent or more manly course.

"We beg leave further to say (since we are reluctantly forced into this allusion to self) that the anti-slavery sentiments, which, from our earliest youth, we imbibed in our native Pennsylvania—the first of the "old thirteen" to abolish slavery—were deepened and strengthened by a residence among slaveholders, and that nowhere, either on slave soil or on free soil, have we expressed other feelings than those of decided hostility to the extension of the withering course.

"Our residence in the South gave us, we hope, the advantage of a thorough comprehension of the question of slavery in all its aspects and of the views of the men who sustain it. It taught us, among other things, that slaveholders, whilst wholly unreasonable and even perfidious in their aggressions upon freedom, have yet the magnanimity to despise a Nothern traitor; and that all organists and apologists of *dough-facery*, after earning the contempt of freeman at home, have only for consolation the *kicks* and *cuffs* of their Southern masters.

"But we forbear; the opinion now current is that our neighbors of the *Age*, in consenting to preach *acquiescence* under the "crushing out" process of Pierce and Cushing, went it *dirt cheap*, and have even failed to receive the whole of the stipulated compensation. Under this belief the derision which they so richly merited and at first so bountifully received is rapidly subsiding and giving place

CHAPTER IV.

AN EDITOR.

THE strictly journalistic career of James G. Blaine may be said to have extended over six years, from 1854 to 1860. It was in the former year that he severed his connection with the Institution of the Blind in Philadelphia, and moved to Augusta, Maine, the former home of his wife.

The two great parties of the time were the Whigs and the Democrats. There were ominous movements in Congress; there were doubtful fears surrounding and darkening the doors of the White House. The Missouri Compromise, the Lecompton Constitution, the blood poured upon the soil of Kansas, the admission of certain States, the triumphs and treacheries of the Whigs, the distrusts and successes of the Democracy, were the incidents of the years just preceding Mr. Blaine's entry into journalism and the years just following.

We recall thus briefly the great and involved issues of the hour in order that the reader may see exactly what labor lay before the young journalist when he grasped his pen to grapple with these questions and to give forth no uncertain sound. And it should be remembered also that at that time the attention paid to the editorial, and the influence carried in the editorial, were far greater and farther-reaching than is possible to-day, in this era of newspapers and not newspaper men. At that time the editorial was the personality of the editor, to-day it is only so in the columns of very few of the existing journals; then the editor was the real leader in a fight; people waited to see what he said, and, no matter the length of his editorial, *they read it through!*

At the time of his arrival in Maine the *Kennebec Journal* was the leading paper in the valley of the river, and owned by William H. Wheeler and William H. Simpson. Wheeler was originally the editor, but he sold his interest to Simpson, who in turn sold to Joseph Baker, a lawyer of Augusta, who stood in need of an editor. The paper was a weekly, with tri-weekly editions during the session of the Legislature. In young Blaine, Baker found a suitable associate, and through the means of his brother-in-law, Jacob Stanwood, the name of "Baker and Blaine" appeared at the head of its columns. This was really Blaine's first natural outlet. In college he had been no mean essayist, and his controversialism had been marked. He had decided views and pronounced ability. His habit of thought suited the editorial chair. New ambitions and hopes quickly dawned on him. An era of influence set in. His latent powers of mind and character soon began to be seen and understood. So marked was his advent that in a very short while he was personally known to every man in Augusta. His stirring editorials became the town talk. His development into a strong, pointed, influential writer was phenomenal.

On taking charge of the paper, the leader entitled "Our Future Course" thus outlined the policy of the paper:—

"Politically, *The Journal* will pursue the same course it has marked out for the last two months. We shall cordially support the Morrill or Republican party, the substantial principles of which are, as we understand them: freedom, temperance, river and harbor improvement within

Constitutional limits, homesteads for freemen, and a just administration of the public lands of the State and nation. We shall advocate the cause of popular education as the surest safeguard of our Republican institutions, and especially the common schools of the State and city. . . . We shall devote a department of our paper each week to religious intelligence of all kinds, and desire that our friends of all denominations will consider themselves invited freely to communicate anything in this department which they wish to have made public, particularly notices of religious conventions, ordinations and meetings of such kind."

It is a most interesting study to look back over the files of Blaine's paper, and mark how, day by day, he developed from an unknown stranger, and unsophisticated youth, into the strong writer and able thinker. Until then all his powers were kept in abeyance.

Selections of the following paragraphs from his early editorials and reports will show the bent of his genius.

Speaking of the organization of the Legislature of Maine, in 1855, he said:

"Thus is the great Republican party of Maine fairly inaugurated into power in the Legislative departments of the State, with a popular good will, a prestige of success, and the elements of permanency such as no party has had since the birth of our State. Long may it live to protect our interests, develop our resources, and *under all circumstances dare to do right, and trust the consequences to Infinite Wisdom.* Let it be not merely the inauguration of a new party, but the exhaltation of principle above party, and the embodiment of honesty into the administration of the State. Then will the honest and good of all classes rally around it, rejoice in it and perpetuate it."

In one place an unjust and foolish judge is said to have charged the Grand Jury of honest men, that they ought to indite some men of the opposite political party for holding secret meetings, whereupon Blaine quaintly remarks: "The Grand Jury listened to the judge with profound attention, and responded, ahem!"

"There might be some reason in the counsel to compromise where the issue is not one of morals, or is doubtful and undefined, but when asked to compromise with an undisguised, opened, hideous wrong like slavery! Never."

"Ought a nation, in strict justice, to be measured by a moral standard different from that which determines the character of a man?"

"All arrows dipped in bad rum or the poison of slander will fall powerless at the moral man's feet."

"In the old country, it is said, everybody is trying to find out what his ancestors were *by birth*, instead of what he himself is by nature. This is certainly the fittest way possible to make a fool of any man who has not had the misfortune to be born one."

"Slavery is sectional and temporary, freedom is national and universal."

"Always revert to the plain facts, and view them separate from all party and sectional influences."

One or two items like the following extract show that Blaine had to meet the usual local prejudice against "Carpetbaggers."

"In reply to the Collector's fierce onslaught upon ourselves, we have not a word to offer. We bow our heads, overcome. The charge of being 'an imported Federalist

CHAPTER V.

IN THE MAINE LEGISLATURE.

As already intimated the entry of James G. Blaine into politics was but natural. If a born editor, he was no less a born politician. There had been a grave political departure from old methods and lines of thought. The formative period of a new party was on, and had to be passed through. The craft when launched had to be manned and navigated. Here was grand opportunity for the vigor and pertinacity of youth, sublime occupation for genius, glowing promise for ambition. It would have been almost impossible for a man of Blaine's organization to escape the enthusiasm inspired by the situation. His youth, his talent, his being, as it were, fitted exactly in with the demands of the hour, and the crisis in turn demanded just such energies as he possessed. To be silent and inert was not to be himself. And no common place would do. He thought, he acted, vigorously, persistently, therefore he led, broadening the plain for his forces as he sped along at the head of victorious columns.

He entered the public arena while yet an editor, and as a delegate to the Republican National Convention in 1856, though he had previously served as secretary of a Republican mass meeting in Augusta, and had participated in some of the initial conventions of the party in the State. In that National Convention, in which John C. Fremont was nominated as Presidential candidate, he was one of the secretaries, and upon his return home found himself

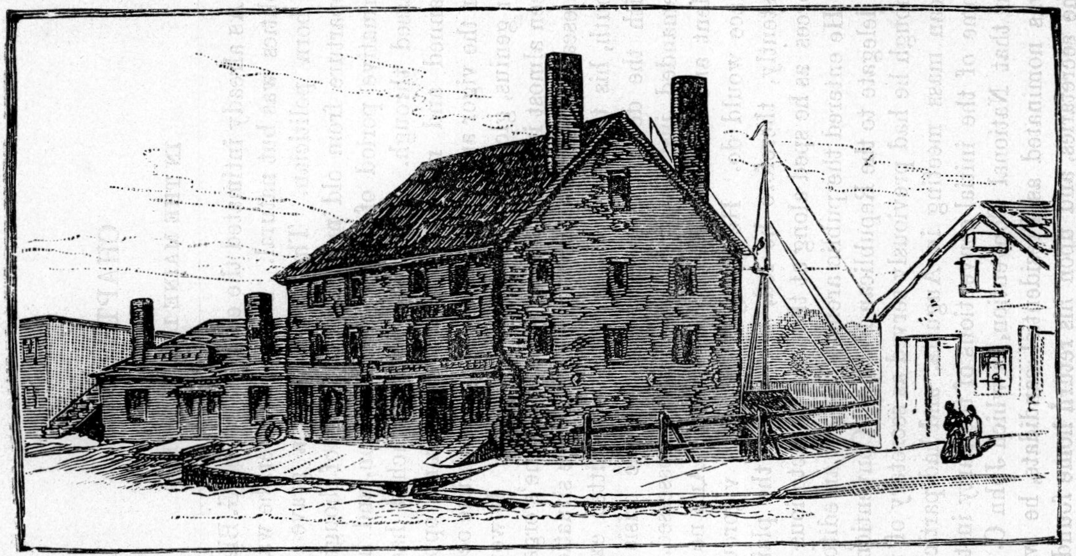

BUILDING WHERE BLAINE WAS EMPLOYED AS A JOURNALIST IN 1855.

called upon to deliver a speech at a ratification meeting. He was but twenty-six years old, and as yet unused to facing large public audiences. We can best describe the situation in the language of an eye witness:—

"At that time he had exhibited all the qualifications of an orator, but had never ventured upon the public platform. He seemed to have a strong fear of addressing a public audience, and it was only after much persuasion that he consented, on this occasion, to speak. When he arose to his feet he was in such a state of perturbation and embarrassment that it was some time before he was able to command himself so as to begin to talk. From the moment he got possession of his voice he continued, and made one of the finest speeches he ever made in his life."

And another writer, also an eye witness, describes the situation more in detail:—

"Among the interesting earlier incidents of Mr. Blaine's political career, was his election as a delegate from the third Congressional district to the first Republican National Convention, in June, 1856, which nominated Gen. John C. Freemont to the Presidency. Upon his return from the convention a ratification meeting was held in Meonian Hall, Augusta, and upon the urgent insistence of some of his personal friends he was persuaded, reluctantly, to appear upon the platform and make report of the doings of the Convention. This was his first public effort. He was then twenty-six years of age. Although remarkably ready and easy of speech and holding a practiced and powerful pen, he had an almost unconquerable repugnance to letting his voice be heard, except in familiar conversation where his brilliant powers of statement and argument, his marvelous memory of dates and events in political history, and his acquaintance with, and keen

called upon to deliver a speech at a ratification meeting. He was but twenty-six years old, and as yet unused to facing large public audiences. We can best describe the situation in the language of an eye witness:—

"At that time he had exhibited all the qualifications of an orator, but had never ventured upon the public platform. He seemed to have a strong fear of addressing a public audience, and it was only after much persuasion that he consented, on this occasion, to speak. When he arose to his feet he was in such a state of perturbation and embarrassment that it was some time before he was able to command himself so as to begin to talk. From the moment he got possession of his voice he continued, and made one of the finest speeches he ever made in his life."

And another writer, also an eye witness, describes the situation more in detail:—

"Among the interesting earlier incidents of Mr. Blaine's political career, was his election as a delegate from the third Congressional district to the first Republican National Convention, in June, 1856, which nominated Gen. John C. Freemont to the Presidency. Upon his return from the convention a ratification meeting was held in Meonian Hall, Augusta, and upon the urgent insistence of some of his personal friends he was persuaded, reluctantly, to appear upon the platform and make report of the doings of the Convention. This was his first public effort. He was then twenty-six years of age. Although remarkably ready and easy of speech and holding a practiced and powerful pen, he had an almost unconquerable repugnance to letting his voice be heard, except in familiar conversation where his brilliant powers of statement and argument, his marvelous memory of dates and events in political history, and his acquaintance with, and keen estimate of the public men and parties of the day, were the delight and wonder of all who listened to him. The writer well recalls the trepidation, at once painful and ludicrous, with which he rose to address the meeting. In confronting the sea of faces, almost every one of whom was known to him, he seemed to be struggling to master the terror that possessed him. He turned pale and red by turns, and almost tottering to the front, stood trembling until the generous applause which welcomed him had died away, when, by supreme effort he broke the spell, at first by the utterance of some hesitating words of greeting and thanks, and then gathering confidence, went on with a speech which stirred the audience as with the sound of a trumpet, and held all present in breathless interest and attention to its close. From that moment Mr. Blaine took rank among the most effective popular speakers of the day; but it may be doubted if among the many maturer efforts of his genius and eloquence upon the political platform or in the legislative tribune, he has ever excited an audience to a more passionate enthusiasm or left a profounder impression upon the minds and hearts of his hearers."

Mr. Blaine's speech upon this occasion is such a valuable contribution to the political literature of the day, and is so important as showing his command of history and his method of thought, that his biography would be incomplete without it. We therefore give it in full. It was delivered in Litchfield, Me., June 28, 1856, and the theme was:

"NOMINATION OF FREEMONT FOR PRESIDENT."

FELLOW-CITIZENS,—The Republican party is a new political organization. It is not yet two years old. Its first small meetings were held late in the summer of 1854, when the name was adopted, and the party organized on the one great principle of resisting the spread of slavery into the Territories of the United States. The new party had its origin in the deep and abiding conviction on the part of the opponents of slavery that the propagandists of the South cannot be trusted upon any adjustment or upon any agreement. Pressed hard by opposition, to-day, they will agree to a compromise; and, to-morrow, if they see opportunity for fresh aggression, they will disregard it and trample upon it. The two great compromises on the subject of slavery were that which established the geographical line of 36° 30′ in the year 1820, known as the Missouri Compromise, and that which was enacted thirty years later and is known as the Compromise of 1850. At both junctures, the potent agency that wrought on behalf of the South was the fear that the Union might be dissolved. That was the threat of Southern leaders; it was the conclusive argument that induced Northern men to yield. But in 1854 the Missouri Compromise was repealed, and, with it, the Compromise of 1850 was put under foot. The division line (by which it was agreed that freedom should have sway north of it and slavery should permissively exist south of it) was destroyed, after thirty-four years of honorable observance on both sides.

"The destruction of the Whig party was one of the immediate results of the repeal of the Missouri Compromise, because the Northern Whigs were largely anti-slavery in feeling, and could not be held in co-operation with a party whose Southern members had broken faith in their zeal for the spread of slavery. A large number of Northern Democrats were equally resolved not to stand by their old party. These two great bodies, joining with the old Free-soil and Liberty party, are the elements that have coalesced and become unified within the ranks of the Republican party. I think it is not boastful to say that in the character of the men who lead this party and of the vast number who compose it, that in its growth, in its zeal, in its unselfish devotion to a single great issue, it is unprecedented, if not phenomenal. It has grown so rapidly that it is in the National field with full strength and with organization—courageous enough to enter the fight, with the conscience and the nerve to accept defeat and prepare for another battle. Its members are not to be put down by the cry of sectionalism or frightened by the threat of disunion. Certainly no member of the Republican party underates the value of the Union of the States, or would hesitate at any sacrifice to preserve it, except the sacrifice of honor, or the sacrifice of that freedom which the Union was established to preserve. But we do not contemplate the dissolution of the Union as a possibility; and certainly no sane man believes that a great body of States, bound together in mutual interest and cemented by a thousand ties, can be torn asunder so readily and so easily as the flippant threats of the Southern extremists would imply.

"The Republican party, therefore, will march forward in the line of duty, and will try to engraft its principles upon the government of the country. They have no purpose to interfere with slavery in the States; they have no purpose to interfere with slavery anywhere, except to the extent that Thomas Jefferson and the Fathers of the Republic interfered with it when they excluded it from free territory. If, indirectly, that policy interfers with slavery in the States, we are not responsible. Certainly the great evil of slavery, wherever it exists, is not to be countenanced and upheld by subjecting other communities and other territory to a like curse. I have no doubt that the great majority of the Republican party would interfere with slavery in the States, if they considered that they had the Constitutional right to do so; but they will not violate their oaths to observe the Constitution, and they will not strain their consciences to make that seem right which the plain letter of the law forbids. But they believe that their right to exclude slavery from the free Territories is just as clear as their inability to interfere with it in the States; and on that single point, great and far-reaching in its effects, we challenge the Democratic party of the South and of the North to a contest for the government of the country.

"The first National Convention of the Republican party has lately been held in Philadelphia, and this Congressional District did me the honor to send me as one of its delegates to that remarkable assemblage. I am sure that I shall be expected by you, as my constituents, to make some report of what was said and done there, and especially what was done by the Maine delegation. The daily journals have given you the details of the proceedings, and I content myself with some general observations on the character of the Convention—its personal character, if I may use the phrase. In the various delegations that composed the Convention, in the sacred cause which it assembled to uphold, and in the work which it accomplished, it will fairly rank as one of the most significant and important political conventions ever held in the United States. A marked feature was the large proportion of young men among its members, and in the general tendency to select that class I can find the only cause for conferring upon me the distinction of membership in such a body.

CHAPTER VI.

IN THE THIRTY-EIGHTH CONGRESS.

In the year 1862, Anson P. Morrill, who had served a term in the Kennebec, or Third Maine, Congressional District, declined to be a candidate for re-election. This left the field open to all competitors, and there was but little hesitation in making a choice. Even before the nominating convention met, all signs pointed to the nomination of James G. Blaine. The times were perilous, the hearts of the people were agitated by events connected with the progress of the war, the constituency of the Third District were intelligent and intensely loyal. They demanded a strong, earnest, aggressive man, and they felt that Blaine had been sufficiently proved to fill their ideal of a Representative in Congress. When the Congressional Convention met at Waterville, on July 8th, 1862, Mr. Blaine received a unanimous nomination. He accepted the honor in an appropriate and eloquent speech, as follows:—

"Mr. Chairman and Gentlemen of the Convention,—I am here to acknowledge with sincere thanks the honor which you have conferred upon me by selecting me as your candidate for Representative in the Thirty-eighth Congress. The unanimity of your action is to me one of its most embarrassing features, for it implies a confidence in my fitness for the position which I myself may well distrust. I can only pledge my best intentions and my most earnest efforts to serve this constituency faithfully and zealously, should the nomination this day made be ratified at the polls.

"The Kennebec District—the name which this county has always given to the Congressional District in which it has been included at each decennial apportionment—has established a character at home and abroad which is difficult to live up to. The distinguished gentleman who now represents it (and whose voluntary retirement gives you this opportunity to place me under deep obligation by the bestowment of your confidence) has won great and important victories on hard-fought political fields, and, in connection with the present Vice-President of the United States, has done more than any other living man to overthrow the Democratic party of Maine. He retires from public life full of honors, and with the unstinted confidence and attachment of the Republicans of the entire State.

"But long before Mr. Morrill's participation in political affairs, the old Kennebec District had won great prominence in Congress by the ability, the ripe culture, the superb talent for debate exhibited by two gentlemen who represented it from 1825 to 1841—Peleg Sprague and George Evans. I see before me gray-haired men whose political activity is stirred afresh by the memory of the contests they waged in this district under the leadership of those young men—for each was in his early thirties when called to lead the National Republican forces against the Democratic dynasty of Jackson and Van Buren.

"Nor should I fail to name the able editor, the sincere friend, the judicious adviser, the upright man, Luther Severance, who after promoting the elections of Mr. Sprague and Mr. Evans with unsurpassed activity and zeal, was rewarded with succession to the seat to which they had given eminent distinction. If you will pardon the personal reference, I regarded it as the chief honor of my life, before you crowned me with your favor to-day, that I followed Luther Severance, *longo intervallo*, in the editorship of the *Kennebec Journal*, which he had founded and nurtured, and to which he had given character and prominence throughout the State. There have perhaps been more brilliant men in Maine than Luther Severance, but not one who ever enjoyed the public confidence in a higher degree or repaid that confidence more amply by an honorable and stainless life.

"It is not wise for candidates to indulge in profuse promises. The Representative must be tested by his acts rather than by his professions. I deem it my duty, however to say that if I am called to a seat in Congress, I shall go there with a determination to stand heartily and unreservedly by the Administration of Abraham Lincoln. In the success of that Administration, under the good Providence of God, rests, I solemnly believe, the fate of the American Union. If we cannot subdue the Rebellion through the agency of the Administration, there is no other power given under Heaven among men to which we can appeal. Hence I repeat, that I shall conceive it to be my duty, as your Representative, to be the unswerving adherent of the policy and measures which the President in his wisdom may adopt. The case is one, in the present exigency, where men loyal to the Union cannot divide. The President is Commander-in-Chief of our land and naval forces, and while he may be counseled he must not be opposed. It is well to recall the lesson of that adage which teaches that one bad general is better than two good ones. Let us then discourage divisions and encourage harmony.

"In this way alone, gentlemen, can we preserve that unity of action among the loyal people so essential to the

the personal reference, I regarded it as the chief honor of my life, before you crowned me with your favor to-day, that I followed Luther Severance, *longo intervallo*, in the editorship of the *Kennebec Journal*, which he had founded and nurtured, and to which he had given character and prominence throughout the State. There have perhaps been more brilliant men in Maine than Luther Severance, but not one who ever enjoyed the public confidence in a higher degree or repaid that confidence more amply by an honorable and stainless life.

"It is not wise for candidates to indulge in profuse promises. The Representative must be tested by his acts rather than by his professions. I deem it my duty, however, to say that if I am called to a seat in Congress, I shall go there with a determination to stand heartily and unreservedly by the Administration of Abraham Lincoln. In the success of that Administration, under the good Providence of God, rests, I solemnly believe, the fate of the American Union. If we cannot subdue the Rebellion through the agency of the Administration, there is no other power given under Heaven among men to which we can appeal. Hence I repeat, that I shall conceive it to be my duty, as your Representative, to be the unswerving adherent of the policy and measures which the President in his wisdom may adopt. The case is one, in the present exigency, where men loyal to the Union cannot divide. The President is Commander-in-Chief of our land and naval forces, and while he may be counseled he must not be opposed. It is well to recall the lesson of that adage which teaches that one bad general is better than two good ones. Let us then discourage divisions and encourage harmony.

"In this way alone, gentlemen, can we preserve that unity of action among the loyal people so essential to the

At the Age of Thirty-five.

maintenance of our Nationality. That unity once broken, we can have no well-founded hope of success. We hear a great deal of talk about the base of operations in the war; at one time on the Rappahannock River, at another on the York, and at still another on the James. But there is one base of operations stronger than all these, and that is on the united hearts and the united action of the loyal people in these States. That once destroyed, all other bases of operation are gone.

"The great object with us all is to subdue the Rebellion—speedily, effectually, finally. In our march to that end we must crush all intervening obstacles. If slavery, or any other "institution," stands in the way, it must be removed. Perish all things else, the National life must be saved. My individual convictions of what may be needful are perhaps in advance of those entertained by some, and less radical than those conscientiously held by others. Whether they are the one or the other, however, I do not wish to see an attempt made to carry them out until it can be done by an Administration sustained by the resistless energy of the loyal masses. I think myself those masses are rapidly adopting the idea that to smite the Rebellion its malignant cause must be smitten, and that to preserve the Union all agencies willing to work for its preservation must be freely and energetically used. That, I believe, is the conclusion which, in due time, the Nation will reach. Perhaps we are slow in coming to it, and it may be that we are even now receiving our severe chastisement for not more readily accepting the teachings of Providence. But it was the tenth plague which softened the heart of Pharoah and caused him to let the oppressed go free. That plague was the sacrifice of the first-born in each household. With the sanguinary battle-fields of Virginia whose records of death we are

CHAPTER VII.

IN THE THIRTY-NINTH CONGRESS.

THE first session of the Thirty-Ninth Congress opened on Dec. 4th, 1865, and closed on July 28th, 1866. Much had transpired between the two sessions to gladden the country and to sadden it. Lee had surrendered on April 9th, 1865. President Lincoln had fallen a victim to the assassin's pistol on April 14th, 1865. Grave doubts overhung the country as to the policy of Andrew Johnson. The period of reconstruction was upon the nation, with all its entanglements.

The favorable turn the rebellion had taken in the autumn of 1864 and the emphatic indorsement of the Lincoln administration, had increased the Republican majority in both Houses of the Thirty-Ninth Congress. The Republicans had a majority of twenty-nine in the Senate and 105 in the House. Schuyler Colfax was re-elected Speaker. Mr. Blaine began to make his presence felt from the very beginning of this session. It was known that none of the younger members had been on more cordial or confidential terms with Mr. Lincoln than the new member from Maine. Towards the expiration of Mr. Lincoln's first term Mr. Blaine was the person with whom the President constantly conferred in regard to political movements in Maine. Ward H. Lamon, Lincoln's law partner, was presented at a conference when Mr. Lincoln requested Mr. Blaine to go to Maine and watch the movements of the President's opponents. The acquaintance between Lincoln and Blaine had begun in Illinois during the Douglas campaign in 1858, and at that early time the Maine editor had predicted in the columns of his paper that Lincoln would be defeated for senator by Douglas, but that he would beat Douglas for president in 1860. A copy of this prophecy Mr. Lincoln carried in his memorandum-book long after he had been inaugurated as president. In 1860, a delegate to the Chicago Convention, Mr. Blaine had been almost the only New England man who had supported Mr. Lincoln from the start, and it is not too much to say that it was Mr. Blaine's early and firm stand for Lincoln which opened the way to the first nomination of the first martyr President.

It is needless to say that Mr. Blaine participated with his usual ardor and ability in all the leading measures of this important session, and aided materially in saving the legislation adequate to the hour, by the passage of bills over President Johnson's vetoes. Thus were saved the amended Freedman's Bureau Bill and the one providing education and military protection for the negro race. Similarly, was passed the Civil Rights Bill, but in a form which led leading statesmen to think that its substance could only be preserved in the form of a Constitutional amendment. This led to the framing and adoption of the Fourteenth amendment to the Constitution, pending which Mr. Blaine made strenuous efforts to have representation based on votables instead of on population, and had the honor of delivering the first speech in the Congress involving the idea. Had his views prevailed there would not have been such a thing as a "Solid South" to-day, based on a representation far in excess of voters, and maintained by depriving hosts of citizens of the franchise accorded to them by the Constitution. His speech was brief and read as follows:—"Were the negroes to be enfranchised throughout the South to-day, no one would insist on the adoption of this amendment; and yet if the amendment shall be incorporated in the Federal Constitution, its incidental evils will abide in the loyal States long after the direct evil which it aims to cure may have been eradicated in the Southern States.

"If voters instead of population shall be made the basis of representation, certain results will follow, not fully appreciated perhaps by some who are now urgent for the change. I will confine my examination of these results to the free States. The ratio of voters to population varies widely in different sections, ranging from a minimum of *nineteen per cent* to a maximum of *fifty-eight per cent*; and the changes which this fact would work in the relative representation of certain States would be monstrous. For example, California has a population of 358,-110, and Vermont 314,369, and each has three representatives on this floor to-day; but California cast 207,000 votes, in electing her three representatives, and Vermont cast 87,000. Assuming voters as the basis of apportionment, and allowing to Vermont three representatives, California would be entitled to eight. The great State of Ohio, with nearly seven times the population of California, would have but little more than two and a half times the number of representatives; and New York, with quite eleven times the population of California, would have in the new style of apportionment less than five times as many members of this House. California it may be said presents an extreme case, but no more so than will continually recur for the next century under the stimulus to the emigration of young voters from the older States to the inviting fields of the Mississippi valley and the Pacific slope.

. . . .

CHAPTER VIII.

IN THE FORTIETH CONGRESS.

THE Fortieth Congress met in extra session on March 5, 1867, pursuant to an act of the previous session. The issues between the Congress and President Johnson had resulted in the choice of 138 Republicans and 47 Democrats in the House. Schuyler Colfax was re-elected Speaker. Political legislation was not the design of the session. It was there for police purposes and to secure a continuity of sessions, which it did by adjournments till the regular session of Dec. 2, 1867. Mr. Blaine took advantage of the situation to make a brief visit to Europe. While absent, what afterward became known as the "Greenback craze" broke out and found advocates among some prominent men, notably Mr. Pendleton and Mr. Butler. Pendleton had introduced a measure looking to the payment of the interest upon U. S. Bonds, and even the principal, in currency, and it had found such able advocates as to quite dumb-found statesmen of a serious turn. Of all national questions those relating to finance were the most difficult to handle prior to the resumption of specie payments. Few indeed were the men equal to the task of laying down and advocating safe, broad-guage principles relative to money, and fewer still were capable of meeting and overthrowing the dangerous plausibilities of those who sought to undermine national credit by making the currency serve illegitimate purposes. It is greatly to Mr. Blaine's credit that he struck the first decisive blow at the undermining effect of Mr. Pendleton's and Mr. Butler's theories. This he did in the extra session of the Fortieth Congress which met Nov. 21, 1867. He had evidently spent much time and research on his speech, and when it came, it not only fell like a blow on his opponents, but electrified the country. The House was in Committee of the whole on the state of the Union, on Nov. 26, 1867, when Mr. Blaine arose and said:—

MR. CHAIRMAN,—Within the past few months, some erroneous and mischievous views have been put forward in regard to the nature of the public obligation imposed by the debt of the United States. Without stopping to notice the lesser lights of the new doctrine, and not caring to analyze the various forms of repudiation suggested from irresponsible sources throughout the country, I propose to review, as briefly as may be, the position contemporaneously assumed by two able and distinguished gentlemen—the one from the West, the other from the East—the one the late candidate of the Democratic party for the Vice-Presidency—[Mr. Pendleton of Ohio]—the other a prominent member of this House from the strongest Republican district of the State of Massachusetts [General Butler].

The position of these gentlemen I understand to be simply this: *that the principal of the United States bonds, known as the five-twenties, may be fairly and legally paid in paper currency by the Government after the expiration of five years from the date of issue.*

"A brief review of the origin of the five-twenty bonds will demonstrate, I think, that this position is in contravention of the honor and good faith of the National Government; that it is hostile to the spirit and the letter of the law; that it contemptuously ignores the common understanding between borrower and lender at the time the loan was negotiated; and that finally, even if such mode of payment were honorable and practicable, it would prove disastrous to the financial interests of the Government and the general prosperity of the country. I crave the attention and the indulgence of the House while I recapitulate the essential facts in support of my assertion.

"The issue of the five-twenty bonds was originally authorized by the act of Feb. 25, 1862, which provided for the large amount of $500,000,000. It is this series which was successfully disposed of by Jay Cooke & Co. in 1863, and of which a great proportion was subsequently purchased by foreign capitalists. It will be borne in mind that up to that time in all the loan bills passed by Congress not one word had ever been said in regard to coin payment either of bond or coupon; and yet it will be equally borne in mind that coin payment, both of the principal and interest of the public debt, has been the invariable rule from the foundation of the government. No instance to the contrary can be found in our history. In the pithy language of Nathaniel Macon, "our Government was a hard-money Government, founded by hard-money men, and its debts were hard-money debts."

"It will be still further borne in mind that when the bill authorizing the original issue of five-twenties was under discussion in Congress no man of any party, either in the Senate or the House, ever intimated that those bonds were to be paid in any thing else than gold or silver. The issue of legal-tender notes of contemporaneous origin was regarded as a temporary expedient, forced upon us by the cruel necessities and demands of war, and it was universally conceded that the specie basis was to be resumed long before the bonds should mature for payment. And

CHAPTER IX.

IN THE FORTY-FIRST CONGRESS; AS SPEAKER OF THE HOUSE.

THE Forty-first Congress was called into extra session by President Grant, on March 4th, 1869. There were large Republican majorities in both Houses, the House standing 149 Republicans to 64 Democrats. The object of the extra session was to secure new legislation respecting the admission of those seceded States, which had refused to ratify the Fourteenth and Fifteenth amendments to the Constitution.

In organizing the House for this delicate work it was necessary to place its ablest parliamentarian in the Speaker's chair. It had lost the efficient services of Mr. Colfax, who had been elected Vice President of the United States. What so natural as to turn to Mr. Blaine in such a crisis. He was thoroughly acquainted with men, the entire field of duty before him, the measures which dominated reconstruction and vitally concerned the national credit, the currency of the country and its commercial welfare. His Republicanism was of the most pronounced type—stalwart to the core. His education as Speaker of the Maine House of Representatives, which had all along availed him much, came to his rescue when in search of the honors of Speaker of the National House. His knowledge of the manual, his recollection of names, his fairness and firmness, his quickness of perception, his ability to expedite business, his wonderful control of self and of exciting situations,

BLAINE'S HOME AT AUGUSTA, ME.

his magnetic qualities of leadership, all conspired to make his candidacy for the Speakership desirable and sure. He was therefore nominated for this important position by acclamation in the Republican caucus of the Forty-first Congress, at its extra session, and was elected by 136 votes as against 57 cast for Mr. Kerr, the Democratic candidate. So efficient did he prove in this difficult position that similar honors awaited him in the Forty-second and Forty-third Congresses.

Ordinarily the brilliant qualities of the member on the floor are obscured by elevation to the Speakership. His identity with public measures is apt to be somewhat lost. But Mr. Blaine's interest in the political measures he had been identified with so long and honorably did not flag. He did what few men are capable of, to wit, win a reputation as a fair and capable parliamentarian, which, if possible, added to the prestige he had achieved on the floor. There really seemed to be no number to the many sides of his qualifications and no bottom to his resources. Emergencies arose thick and fast in those days of momentous questions and fierce party clashes, but he preserved a dignity worthy his high position and met new situations with perfect equipoise. There was that about his ministration which drew the favor of both parties, and proved him a man not only of striking aptitude but remarkable for his ability to control the passions of an assembly and direct its procedure. It was these same qualities in him which passed beyond the limits of Congress and away out to the country, and taught his admirers to look on him as a natural leader of men and as a safe controlling spirit whether in hours of calm or passion. Says a writer, "In the position of Speaker of the House, his quickness of perception, decision of manner, thorough knowledge of parliamentary law and usages, and impartial and judicial

his magnetic qualities of leadership, all conspired to make his candidacy for the Speakership desirable and sure. He was therefore nominated for this important position by acclamation in the Republican caucus of the Forty-first Congress, at its extra session, and was elected by 136 votes as against 57 cast for Mr. Kerr, the Democratic candidate. So efficient did he prove in this difficult position that similar honors awaited him in the Forty-second and Forty-third Congresses.

Ordinarily the brilliant qualities of the member on the floor are obscured by elevation to the Speakership. His identity with public measures is apt to be somewhat lost. But Mr. Blaine's interest in the political measures he had been identified with so long and honorably did not flag. He did what few men are capable of, to wit, win a reputation as a fair and capable parliamentarian, which, if possible, added to the prestige he had achieved on the floor. There really seemed to be no number to the many sides of his qualifications and no bottom to his resources. Emergencies arose thick and fast in those days of momentous questions and fierce party clashes, but he preserved a dignity worthy his high position and met new situations with perfect equipoise. There was that about his ministration which drew the favor of both parties, and proved him a man not only of striking aptitude but remarkable for his ability to control the passions of an assembly and direct its procedure. It was these same qualities in him which passed beyond the limits of Congress and away out to the country, and taught his admirers to look on him as a natural leader of men and as a safe controlling spirit whether in hours of calm or passion. Says a writer, "In the position of Speaker of the House, his quickness of perception, decision of manner, thorough knowledge of parliamentary law and usages, and impartial and judicial mind, added to his clear voice and impressive presence, made him a truly great presiding officer."

When the honors of the Speakership fell to him he was perhaps the youngest man who had ever borne them, being but thirty-nine years old.

On taking the chair Mr. Blaine addressed the House as follows:—

"I thank you profoundly for the great honor which you have just conferred upon me. The gratification which this signal mark of your confidence brings to me finds its only drawback in the diffidence with which I assume the weighty duties devolved upon me. Succeeding to a chair made illustrious by the services of such eminent statesmen and skilled parliamentarians as Clay, and Stevenson, and Polk, and Winthrop, and Banks, and Grow, and Colfax, I may well distrust my ability to meet the just expectations of those who have shown me such marked partiality. But relying, gentlemen, on my honest purpose to perform all my duties faithfully and fearlessly, and trusting in a large measure to the indulgence which I am sure you will always extend to me, I shall hope to retain, as I have secured your confidence, your kindly regard and your generous support.

"The Forty-first Congress assembles at an auspicious period in the history of our government. The splendid and impressive ceremonial which we have just witnessed in another part of the Capitol appropriately symbolizes the triumphs of the past and the hopes of the future. A great chieftain, whose sword, at the head of gallant and victorious armies, saved the Republic from dismemberment and ruin, has been fitly called to the highest civic honor which a grateful people can bestow. Sustained by a Congress that so ably represents the loyalty, the patriotism, and the personal worth of the nation, the President this day inaugurated will assure to the country an administration of purity, fidelity and prosperity; an era of liberty regulated by law, and of law thoroughly inspired with liberty.

"Congratulating you, gentlemen, upon the happy auguries of the day, and invoking the gracious blessing of Almighty God on the arduous and responsible labors before you, I am now ready to take the oath of office and enter upon the discharge of the duties to which you have called me."

So satisfactory did his ministration prove to friend and foe that at the expiration of the Forty-first Congress, March 3, 1871, Mr. S. S. Cox, then of New York, one of his bitterest political opponents and a recognized Democratic leader, offered the following resolution, which was passed:—

"In view of the difficulties involved in the performance of the duties of the presiding officer of this House, and of the able, courteous, dignified and impartial discharge of those duties by Hon. James G. Blaine, during the present Congress, it is eminently becoming that our thanks be and they are hereby tendered to the Speaker thereof."

To this resolution and as part of the adjournment proceedings Mr. Blaine made the following appropriate reply:—

"Our labors are at an end; but I delay the final adjournment long enough to return my most profound and respectful thanks for the commendation which you have been pleased to bestow upon my official course and conduct. In a deliberate body of this character a presiding officer is fortunate if he retains the confidence and steady support of his political associates. Beyond that you give me the assurance that I have earned the good will of those from whom I am separated by party lines. Your expressions

CHAPTER X.

IN THE FORTY-SECOND CONGRESS; AS SPEAKER OF THE HOUSE.

WE have already seen how the House, by its resolution of thanks, saw fit to regard Mr. Blaine's conduct while in the chair during the Forty-First Congress. Nothing can add to the strength and impartiality of a verdict in one's favor when voluntarily rendered by one's foes. President Grant called the Forty-second Congress in extra session March 4, 1871, the object being to amend the enforcement acts so as to more effectually reach the outrages perpetrated in the southern states. The Republican majority was by no means so large as formerly, there being 138 Republicans to 103 Democrats. The House organized by re-electing James G. Blaine as speaker, by a vote of 126, to one of 92 for his competitior Geo. W. Morgan. On being conducted to the chair he addressed the House as follows:—

"The speakership of the American House of Represenlives has always been esteemed as an enviable honor. A re-election to the position carries with it peculiar gratification, in that it implies an approval of past official bearing. For this great mark of your confidence, I can but return to you my sincerest thanks, with the assurance of my utmost devotion to the duties which you call upon me to discharge.

"Chosen by the party representing the political majority in the House, the Speaker owes a faithful allegiance to the principles and policy of that party. But he will fall far below the honorable requirements of his station if he fails to give to the minority their full rights under the rules which he is called upon to administer. The successful working of our grand system of government depends largely upon the vigilance of party organizations, and the most wholesome legislation which this House produces and perfects is that which results from opposing forces mutually eager and watchful and well nigh balanced in numbers.

"The Forty-Second Congress assembles at a period of general content, happiness and prosperity throughout the land. Under the wise administration of the national government peace reigns in all our borders, and the only serious misunderstanding with any foreign power is, we may hope, at this moment in process of honorable, cordial and lasting adjustment. We are fortunate in meeting at such a time, in representing such constituencies, in legislating for such a country.

"Trusting gentlemen, that our official intercourse may be free from all personal asperity, believing that all our labors will eventuate for the public good, and craving the blessing of Him without whose aid we labor in vain, I am now ready to proceed with the further organization of the House; and as the first step thereto, I will myself take the oath prescribed by the Constitution and laws."

It was during this extra session that Mr. Blaine took occasion to show that his occupancy of the Speaker's chair did not necessarily constrain him to silence under the many attacks made upon him by envious or maliciously inclined members. General Butler had indiscreetly charged him with the authorship of a resolution providing, for an investigation into alleged outrages perpetrated upon loyal citizens of the South, and for being responsible for its adoption in a Republican caucus, Mr. Blaine, March 16, 1871, at once left the chair and took the floor in his defence, when the following sharp colloquy ensued, —interesting as showing Mr. Blaine's courage, tact and persistency :—

Mr. Blaine, the Speaker. [Mr. Wheeler, of New York, in the chair.] I desire to ask the gentleman from Massachusetts (Mr. Butler) whether he denies to me the right to have down that resolution?

Mr. Butler. I have made no assertion on that subject one way or the other.

Mr. Blaine. Did not the gentleman distinctly know that I drew it?

Mr. Butler. No, sir.

Mr. Blaine. Did I not take it to the gentleman and read it to him?

Mr. Butler. Yes, sir.

Mr. Blaine. Did I not show him the manuscript?

Mr. Butler. Yes, sir.

Mr. Blaine. In my own handwriting?

Mr. Butler. No, sir.

Mr. Blaine. And at his suggestion I added these words: "And the expenses of said committee shall be paid from the contingent fund of the House of Representatives" [applause], and the fact that ways and means were wanted to pay the expenses was the only objection he made to it.

Mr. Butler. What was the answer the gentleman made? I suppose I may ask that, now that the Speaker has come upon the floor.

Mr. Blaine. The answer was that I immediately wrote the amendment providing for the payment of the expenses of the committee.

Mr. Butler. What was my answer? Was it not that under no circumstances would I have anything to do with it, being bound by the action of the caucus?

Mr. Blaine. No, sir; the answer was that under no circumstances would you serve as chairman.

Mr. Butler. Or have anything to do with the resolution.

Mr. Blaine. There are two hundred and twenty-four members of the House of Representatives. A committee of thirteen can be found without the gentleman from Massachusetts being on it. His service is not essential to the constitution of the committee.

Mr. Butler. Why did you not find such a committee, then?

Mr. Blaine. Because I knew very well that if I omitted the appointment of the gentleman it would be heralded throughout the length and breadth of the country, by the *claquers* who have so industriously distributed this letter this morning, that the Speaker had packed the committee, as the gentleman said he would, with "weak-kneed Republicans," who would not go into an investigation vigorously, as he would. That was the reason. [Applause.] So that the Chair laid the responsibility upon the gentleman of declining the appointment.

Mr. Butler. I knew that was the trick of the Chair.

Mr. Blaine. Ah, the "trick!" We now know what the gentleman meant by the word "trick." I am very glad to know that the "trick" was successful.

Mr. Butler. No doubt.

Mr. Blaine. It is this "trick" which pleases the gentleman from Massachusetts on his responsibility before the country.

Mr. Butler. Exactly.

Mr. Blaine. Wholly.

CHAPTER XI.

IN THE FORTY-THIRD CONGRESS; AS SPEAKER OF THE HOUSE.

THE Forty-third Congress opened in first session, December 1, 1873. The Republican majority was still large, there being 198 Republicans to 91 Democrats. Mr. Blaine was chosen Speaker for the third time by 189 votes against 80 votes cast for all others. On opening the House he delivered the following address:—"The vote this moment announced by the Clerk is such an expression of your confidence as calls for my sincerest thanks. To be chosen Speaker of the American House of Representatives is always an honorable distinction; to be chosen a third time enhances the honor more than three-fold; to be chosen by the largest body that ever assembled in the Capitol imposes a burden of responsibility which only your indulgent kindness could embolden me to assume.

"The first occupant of this Chair presided over a House of sixty-five members, representing a population far below the present aggregate of the State of New York. At that time in the whole United States there were not fifty thousand civilized inhabitants to be found one hundred miles distant from the flow of the Atlantic tide. To-day, gentlemen, a large body of you come from beyond that limit, and represent districts then peopled only by the Indian and adventurous frontiersman. The National Government is not yet as old as many of its

CHAPTER XI.

IN THE FORTY-THIRD CONGRESS; AS SPEAKER OF THE HOUSE.

THE Forty-third Congress opened in first session, December 1, 1873. The Republican majority was still large, there being 198 Republicans to 91 Democrats. Mr. Blaine was chosen Speaker for the third time by 189 votes against 80 votes cast for all others. On opening the House he delivered the following address:—"The vote this moment announced by the Clerk is such an expression of your confidence as calls for my sincerest thanks. To be chosen Speaker of the American House of Representatives is always an honorable distinction; to be chosen a third time enhances the honor more than three-fold; to be chosen by the largest body that ever assembled in the Capitol imposes a burden of responsibility which only your indulgent kindness could embolden me to assume.

"The first occupant of this Chair presided over a House of sixty-five members, representing a population far below the present aggregate of the State of New York. At that time in the whole United States there were not fifty thousand civilized inhabitants to be found one hundred miles distant from the flow of the Atlantic tide. To-day, gentlemen, a large body of you come from beyond that limit, and represent districts then peopled only by the Indian and adventurous frontiersman. The National Government is not yet as old as many of its

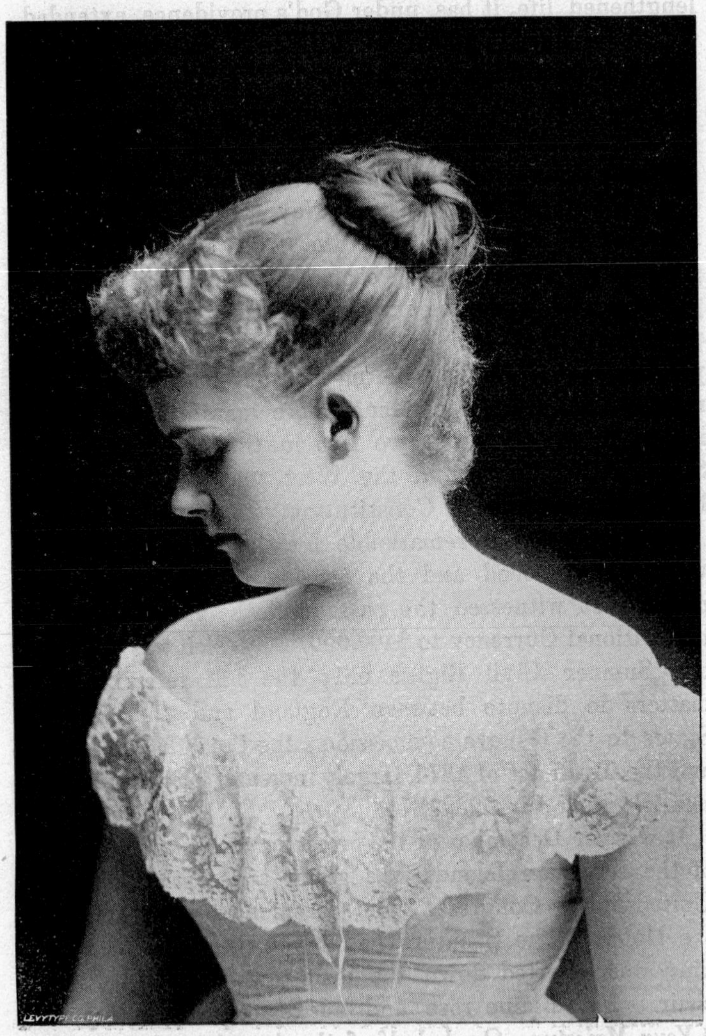

MRS. JAMES G. BLAINE, JR.

citizens; but in this brief span of time, less than one lengthened life, it has, under God's providence, extended its power until a continent is the field of its empire and attests the majesty of its law.

"With the growth of new States and the resulting changes in the centres of population, new interests are developed, rival to the old, but by no means hostile, diverse but not antagonistic. Nay, rather are all these interests in harmony; and the true science of just government is to give to each its full and fair play, oppressing none by undue exaction, favoring none by undue privilege. It is this great lesson which our daily experience is teaching us, binding us together more closely, making our mutual dependence more manifest, and causing us to feel, whether we live in the North or in the South, in the East or in the West, that we have indeed but "one country, one Constitution, one destiny."

The session was remarkable for the large amount of work accomplished and the number of important bills passed. It witnessed the passage of the bill to increase the National Currency to $400,000,000, which was vetoed; the Sumner Civil Rights bill; the bill referring all matters in dispute between England and the United States to the Geneva commission; the Poland Utah Bill; and the Tariff act of 1874, largely increasing duties. The session ended June 23, 1874.

It was in December of the previous year that the King of the Hawaiian Islands was given a reception by the United States Congress. The ceremonies were held in the House. The Senators had taken their seats and the king was escorted down the aisle toward the Speaker's chair. Mr. Blaine rose and addressed his majesty:—
"*Your Majesty:*—On behalf of the American Congress I welcome you to these halls. The Senators from our

States and the Representatives of our people unite in cordial congratulations upon your auspicious journey, and in the expression of the gratification and pleasure afforded by your presence in the Capitol of the Nation as the Nation's guest. Your Majesty's appearance among us is the first instance in which a reigning sovereign has set foot upon the soil of the United States, and it is a significant circumstance that the visit comes to us from the West and not from the East. Probably no single event could more strikingly typify the century's progress in your Majesty's country and in our own than the scene here and now transpiring. The rapid growth of the Republic on its Western coast has greatly enlarged our intercourse with your insular kingdom, and has led us all to a knowledge of your wisdom and beneficence as a ruler, and your exalted virtues as a man. Our whole people cherish for your subjects the most friendly regard. They trust and believe that the relations of the two countries will always be as peaceful as the great sea that rolls between us—uniting and not dividing."

The Administration during 1874 was exceedingly pinched in its Southern policy, and riots which threatened to culminate in a war of races were common in the South. The exposure of the "Whiskey Ring" fell like a pall upon the country, already deeply affected by the panic of 1873 and the hard times which followed—times which had seriously affected the political situation of 1874, had given to the Democrats, under the cry of calamity, a majority in the Forty-fourth Congress, and had reduced Mr. Blaine's majority in his District to 2,830, the smallest he ever received. It stands greatly to Mr. Blaine's credit that he strove with all his energy to stem the current which was running so strongly against his party. His speeches were masterly outlines of the situation and earnest exhortations to firmness and intelligent exercise of rights in an extraordinary hour. He had received from the Republicans of his District his seventh unanimous nomination, and on June 20th, 1874, he thus responded to his nomination:—

"GENTLEMEN,—Permit me to tender my profound acknowledgments to the Republicans of the Kennebec district for their continued manifestation of approval and regard. I have said, very frequently in private, sometimes in public—never, I trust, in a boastful or vainglorious spirit—that I did not believe another Congressional District could be found in the United States superior to the one you empower me to represent, in all the elements of true patriotism; in public and private virtue; in general intelligence and culture, enforced through the common school, the academy and the college; in universal thrift and comfort without large individual wealth; in political conviction firm and steadfast beyond doubt or waver, and yet always tolerant toward those who think differently. Such a constituency confer honor upon any man whom they call to represent them in the National councils, and I beg to make known my grateful appreciation of the trust and confidence which they have so long and so generously reposed in me.

"The resolutions to which you invite my attention are so generally acceptable to the people of the district that no issue will be made on the matters embraced in them. The currency question at one time threatening to divide parties, and, what would be far more serious, to divide sections, is in process of a happy adjustment, partly by wise and temperate enactment passed by a large majority in both branches of Congress and approved by the President, but in a far greater degree by the operation of causes more powerful than any legislation can be. In

CHAPTER XII.

IN THE FORTY-FOURTH CONGRESS; AGAIN ON THE FLOOR.

As intimated, the dread reactions in nature and business, which are comprehended in the word "calamity," had their counterpart in the ascendency of Democracy, in 1874. Democracy has ever been the retroactive agency in the American Republic. Its triumphs have been the correlative of antagonism to Americanism, whether nature chose to assert herself in bad crops, economy in financial distress, or offensive foreign interference in advantages which favored monarchy as against Republican solidarity and experiment. Slavery was not so much slavery as an aim at paid labor, not so much a system as a threat upon honest industry and substantial progress. The war of the Rebellion was not so much a war as a blow at the great Republican experiment and a return to the ideas that dominated Europe and bred arristocratic institutions.

The swash of sentiment in 1874, carried into the House a Democratic majority. The Forty-fourth Congress opened its first session December 6, 1875, with a majority, and organized by the election of Michael C. Kerr, of Indiana, as Speaker. Mr. Blaine, who had presided for six years was thus relegated to the floor. But he did not return to take any second place among the many distinguished members of his—then minority—party. He was the recognized leader of the Republican forces, and such a leadership has never been paralleled. It was a time when the "Rebel Brigadiers," flushed with their return to power, inspired with the belief that Appomattox was to be avenged, angry at everything found on the statute books, and determined to recover by legislation all the ground lost by rebellion, were pressing their eagerly sought, though long postponed, opportunity to the uttermost. The situation called for all of the genius and boldness of such an one as Mr. Blaine in attack, all his versatility in discussion, all his self-possession in the midst of crisis, all his parliamentary wisdom in handling favored measures or baffling ingenious opposition. Through his adroit management and unmatched vigor he compelled a respect for the minority which made it a complete check on the opposition, and as potent in shaping political measures as if it had enjoyed a majority in numbers. Hitherto his career had developed the qualities of statesmanship necessary to success in shaping and advocating the measures of a majority. Men who are great in offensive emergencies often weaken and fail when put on the defensive. But hopefulness and the heroic so abounded in Mr. Blaine's nature that he was, if anything, stronger under the enemy's fire than when he had full command of the field. His vigilance was quickened and his aggressiveness showed at its best. Opposition seemed to present to him his greatest occasion for crushing argument, withering rebuke, or splendid rhetorical flight. It gave full play to those powers of extemporization which, as he has said himself, he never hoped to equal in vividness, grace or vigor, with the pen. To thought, to language, to gesture, to emotion, he added the magnetism of a striking presence, the thrill of burning earnestness, the inspiring consciousness of rectitude. Few have forgotten the sudden tilt by which, in a day, a victorious and exultant Democratic majority was changed into a surprised, subdued, and saddened crowd, under Mr. Blaine's aggressive and unexpected tactics. The debates of that memorable session on the proposition to remove the disabilities of Jefferson Davis are still fresh in all minds, and more likely to be appreciated perhaps to-day than at any time. Mr. Blaine's speeches laid the foundation of success in the campaign of 1876 though he was not selected as the standard-bearer. The excitement growing out of this exciting session with all its attendant events brought Mr. Blaine more prominently before the country than any other citizen for the time, centered upon him indeed a hostility more malignant and a love more enthusiastic than are often inspired by public service, and gave him such a national fame that he at once became a prominent candidate for the Presidency.

It was on the very first day of the session, December 6, 1874, that the Democrats attempted to tear open the Louisiana question, already put to rest by the President, both Houses of Congress, and the people of the State, that Mr. Blaine by his boldness, promptitude and parliamentary skill, turned the tactics of the majority to the account of the minority and served one of the most signal victories ever won in legislative halls.

Within a few days he proposed an amendment to the Constitution prohibiting the sectarian control of public school funds in any State. This was a measure which President Grant highly favored, as evinced by his declarations during a visit to the North-west. It never came up as a political measure, but Mr. Blaine formulated his thoughts respecting it in a letter to a prominent citizen in Ohio, in which he said:—

AUGUSTA, ME., October 20, 1875.

"MY DEAR SIR: The public-school agitation in your late campaign is liable to break out elsewhere, and occurring first in one State and then in another, may keep the whole country in a ferment for years to come. This inevitably arouses sectarian feelings and leads to that bitterest and most deplorable of all strifes, the strife between religious denominations. It seems to me that this question ought to be settled in some definite and comprehensive way, and the only settlement that can be final is the complete victory for non-sectarian schools. I am sure this will be demanded by the American people at all hazards, and at any cost.

"The dread of sectarian legislation in this country has been felt many times in the past. It began very early. The first amendment to the Constitution, the joint production of Jefferson and Madison, proposed in 1789, declared that 'Congress shall make no law respecting an establishment of religion, nor prohibiting the free exercise thereof.' At that time, when the powers of the Federal Government were untried and developed, the fear was that Congress might be the source of danger to perfect religious liberty, and hence all power was taken away from it. At the same time the States were left free to do as they pleased in regard to 'an establishment of religion,' for the tenth amendment proposed by that eminent jurist, Theophilus Parsons, and adopted contemporaneously with the first, declared that 'all powers not delegated to the United States by the Constitution, nor prohibited by it to the States, are reserved to the States respectively, or to the people.'"

"A majority of the people in any State in this Union can, therefore, if they desire it, have an established Church, under which the minority may be taxed for the erection of church-edifices which they never enter, and for the support of which they do not believe. This power was actually exercised in some of the States long after the

CHAPTER XIII.

IN THE SENATE.

On June 10, 1876, just four days before the meeting of the Republican National Convention at Cincinnati, the Governor of Maine appointed Mr. Blaine a United States Senator in place of Hon. Lot M. Morrill who had resigned to take the place of Secretary of the Treasury in President Grant's cabinet. He was, on the meeting of the Legislature, elected to fill Mr. Morrill's unexpired term, which ended March 4, 1877. At the opening of the second term of the Forty-fourth Congress, Dec. 4, 1876, he took his seat in the Senate chamber. In putting off the honors of a Congressional District to accept those of an entire State, he bade farewell to his immediate constituents in the following letter:

"Beginning with 1862 you have by continuous elections sent me as your representative to the Congress of the United States. For such marked confidence I have endeavored to return the most zealous and devoted service in my power, and it is certainly not without a feeling of pain that I now surrender a trust by which I have always felt so signally honored. It has been my boast in public and in private that no man on the floor of Congress ever represented a constituency more distinguished for intelligence, for patriotism, for public and personal virtue. The cordial support you have so uniformly given me through these fourteen eventful years is the chief honor of my life. In closing the intimate relations I have so long held with

JAMES G. BLAINE, JR.

the people of this district it is a great satisfaction to me to know that with returning health I shall enter upon a field of duty in which I can still serve them in common with the larger constituency of which they form a part."

The old *Kennebec Journal*, which had witnessed his entrance into editorial life, and whose pages had often been made to glow with his illuminating pen, returned as an answer from his constituents and the people of the entire State the following:

"Fourteen years ago, standing in the Convention at which he was first nominated, Mr. Blaine pledged himself to use his best services for the district, and to support to the best of his ability the policy of Abraham Lincoln to subdue the rebellion, and then and there expressed plainly the idea that slavery must and ought to be abolished to save the Union. That he has kept his pledge faithfully his constituents know and feel, and the records of Congress attest. To this district his abilities were freely given, and as he rose in honor in the House and in the public estimation he reflected honor and gave strength to the constituency that supported him. Every step he made in advance was a gain for them. It was a grand thing for this district to have as its Representative in Congress for six years the Speaker of the House, filling the place next in importance to that of President of the United States, with matchless ability. It was a grander thing when he took the lead of the minority in the House last December, routed the Democratic majority, and drove back in dismay the ex-Confederates who were intending and expecting through the advantage they had already gained to grasp the supreme power in the nation and wield it in the interest of the cause of secession and rebellion revived. For what he has done as their Representative in Congress, never will this Third District of Maine forget to honor the

the people of this district it is a great satisfaction to me to know that with returning health I shall enter upon a field of duty in which I can still serve them in common with the larger constituency of which they form a part."

The old *Kennebec Journal*, which had witnessed his entrance into editorial life, and whose pages had often been made to glow with his illuminating pen, returned as an answer from his constituents and the people of the entire State the following:

"Fourteen years ago, standing in the Convention at which he was first nominated, Mr. Blaine pledged himself to use his best services for the district, and to support to the best of his ability the policy of Abraham Lincoln to subdue the rebellion, and then and there expressed plainly the idea that slavery must and ought to be abolished to save the Union. That he has kept his pledge faithfully his constituents know and feel, and the records of Congress attest. To this district his abilities were freely given, and as he rose in honor in the House and in the public estimation he reflected honor and gave strength to the constituency that supported him. Every step he made in advance was a gain for them. It was a grand thing for this district to have as its Representative in Congress for six years the Speaker of the House, filling the place next in importance to that of President of the United States, with matchless ability. It was a grander thing when he took the lead of the minority in the House last December, routed the Democratic majority, and drove back in dismay the ex-Confederates who were intending and expecting through the advantage they had already gained to grasp the supreme power in the nation and wield it in the interest of the cause of secession and rebellion revived. For what he has done as their Representative in Congress, never will this Third District of Maine forget to honor the name of James G. Blaine. It will live in the hearts of this people even as the name of Henry Clay is still loved by the people of his old district in Kentucky."

Mr. Blaine's great prominence in public affairs, his identity and familiarity with leading political, financial and industrial questions, the conspicuous and trusted position he occupied in his party, made his transfer from the House to the Senate as easy as it was natural. In this body of men of greater age and dignity, and amid discussions supposably graver, more deliberate and more learned than those of the House, he was from the first a peer. Contrary to the traditions which gave a monopoly of the debates to the older members, he often came forward with his own original and electric views, to which as respectful a hearing was accorded as though he had been one of the oldest and most privileged members.

He was subsequently elected his own successor in the Senate for the term beginning March 4, 1877, and ending March 3, 1883. When the second session of the Forty-fourth Congress met, December 4, 1876, Mr. Blaine took his seat in the Senate Chamber. The question of the hour which dominated all others and occupied almost the entire time of the session was the disputed Electoral count. The inadequacy of all laws regulating the count of presidential electors was painfully manifest. The country suddenly found itself on the verge of a crisis and a single false step might have precipitated an outbreak. All the passions of the presidential campaign were carried over to the Congress. The Republicans claimed that the President of the Senate had, under the law, the sole right to open and announce the returns in the presence of the two Houses. The Democrats claimed that the two Houses acting as a joint body could control the count under the law, and some Democrats even went so far as to say that

CHAPTER XIV.

THE CONVENTION OF 1876.

THE troubles in the South and the almost universal overthrow of the prevailing, or "Carpetbag," State governments, led to the belief that the presidential campaign of 1876 would be an exceedingly close one. The Greenback party bade fair to be an important factor in the North, and a source of weakness to both parties. It was in the field as early as May 17th with its nominees. Grant had been spoken of by the Republicans for a third term, but so pronounced was the sentiment against this that the House of Representatives and a Republican State Convention in Pennsylvania declared that a third term for President would be against the "unwritten law" and the traditions. His name was not presented to the Republican Convention, which assembled in Cincinnati on June 14, 1876.

We have already enumerated the conditions and events which pointed to James G. Blaine as the coming candidate of his party for the Presidency in 1876. His popularity and strength with the masses was phenomenal. His reputation as a Statesman was of the highest order. Perhaps he was too independently organized to attach that importance to party discipline and to the use of definite machinery which is not without its effect, and is sometimes necessary, in order to insure success in political conventions, especially those of a national type. Yet there gathered about him a numerous band of admiring and faithful lieutenants, who had been active in all the States and to whom he might well entrust his political fortunes. As sentiment chystalized within the Republican ranks preparatory to the National Convention of 1876, it became clear that Mr. Blaine would have, as his strongest opponents in the Convention, Oliver P. Morton, B. H. Bristow, Roscoe Conkling, John F. Hartranft, and Rutherford B. Hayes, nearly all of whom claimed to have solid State delegations at their back, under what was known as the "unit rule" of voting, that is, voting the States solidly, where a majority of the delegates so willed, instead of permitting each individual delegate to vote his preference. With all this array of strength and talent against him, Mr. Blaine had still a most decided lead, certainly so far as the sentiment of his party was concerned, and assuredly so, provided the delegates chosen were not denied the right to give individual expression of their choice.

Thus matters shaped up until a short time before the Convention, when the Democratic House of Representatives began to give its investigation a turn personal to Mr. Blaine, and to open the flood-gates of abuse in the shape of the "Mulligan Letters," and the inuendoes and falsehoods which accompanied them. We have already seen how promptly and manfully Mr. Blaine met all those charges and how fully he vindicated himself at the bar of honest public opinion. It is doubtful if they served the purpose of changing the course of any of Mr. Blaine's adherents, so prompt and complete was his refutation of them. But they may have affected what might have become the general polity of the Convention in case of a close ballot. Had things taken such shape as that, the nomination being in doubt, Mr. Blaine's candidacy should have resolved itself into one of expediency, the charges might have worked his defeat. Be this as it may, the worst they did was to put Mr. Blaine on the defensive at a most inopportune time. They distracted his attention from his canvass, consumed his time in forcing him to watch and defend his interests as a Representative in Congress, provoked him to tantalizing discussions and exhausted him physically by arduous application, for the time was short in which to provide defence and carry on a winning battle.

It is possible that Mr. Blaine's exertions, and his anxiety of mind, at this time, contributed to the physical blow he was to experience. It was June 11th, four days before the opening of the Convention, that he fell a victim to sun-stroke in Washington, and while on his way to church. He was taken to his residence, and his sudden illness gave rise to great excitement and all sorts of sensational rumors. The effect of the news of his indisposition on the country, and especially upon his supporters, then rallying to his banner in Cincinnati, was startling. Sympathy came from all sources and in such forms as to show the deep hold he had on the affections of the people. His political friends seemed to draw closer about him and to resolve anew to fight his battle to the end. He soon rallied from his attack, and his name went before the Convention, as if the unfortunate blow had not fallen; indeed it may be said that the ardor of his supporters was intensified in proportion to their solicitude for his physical condition and their thankfulness for his speedy convalescence. By June 14 he was sufficiently recovered to telegraph to Mr. Hale at Cincinnati as follows:—

"HON. EUGENE HALE, *Cincinnati:* I am entirely convalescent, suffering only from physical weakness. Impress upon my friends the great depth of gratitude I feel for the

CHAPTER XV.

THE CONVENTION OF 1880.

THE general effect of President Hayes' administration had been to strengthen a growing independent sentiment in the Republican party. Yet this had not operated so as to materially subtract from the strength or popularity of the recognized leaders of the party. On the contrary, it may have contributed to the hardening of party lines in some localities, as it certainly did to a firmer control by leaders, who found themselves with an opportunity in hand.

Long before the date of the National convention the Republican party became the victim of two forces, each exceedingly active and aggressive. The one inclined to a re-nomination of General Grant, whose popularity they would turn to account and with whose strength they would counterbalance the, to them, many weaknesses of the Hayes administration. They were confident that General Grant, who had just returned from his "Tour around the World," had such a hold on the affections of his countrymen as to warrant the risk of his candidacy for a third, though not consecutive, term.

The other force was that which represented an equal stalwartism, and naturally chrystalized about Mr. Blaine. It found its food in admiration for the man, in a desire to retrieve the defeat at Cincinnati by a success at Chicago, in antagonism to the third term idea, and in the faith that Blaine would prove a winning candidate and an ideal President.

As these forces organized and solidified preparatory to the convention, it was seen that a gigantic struggle impended. The Grant force was handled most dexterously and determinedly throughout. The Blaine force, trusting more to the popular spirit, and to the efficacy of spontaneity, postponed its exhibions of skill till the time of the convention. Perhaps its most direct, certainly best organized, show of strength was in the anti-Grant mass-meeting held at Chicago, on the eve of the convention, at which the most radical utterances were loudly applauded, "boss rule" was bitterly denounced, and the idea of a third term utterly repudiated. If applause for a favorite meant anything, the Blaine force was certainly given an impetus, on that occasion, which might well render it irresistible.

The interests of General Grant fell to the keeping of three leaders in three great States—Senators Roscoe Conkling of New York, Cameron of Pennsylvania, and Logan of Illinois. Their alliance was firm and aggressive, and their knowledge of political methods perfect. They had secured the instructions of their respective State conventions for Grant, though not without protest, and with the intention to apply the "unit rule," which the Cincinnati convention had cast aside.

The convention assembled in the Auditorium at Chicago on June 5, 1880. Excitement ran high, and the convention was regarded as one of the most important in the history of the Republican party, involving as it did so many mooted questions of method and polity, which could only be settled after a severe struggle. The Grant forces were thoroughly committed to the "unit rule" as their only hope. The Blaine forces, and the forces of the field, were opposed to it, as their only hope. The Republican National Committee met at the Palmer House prior to the opening of the convention. Senator Cameron was chairman, and he announced his intention of adhering to the "unit rule." A majority of the committee was against him, but Mr. Cameron, by his rulings, thwarted their efforts to deprive him of the right to designate a temporary chairman of the convention. The committee then threatened to remove Mr. Cameron from the chairmanship, but this radical measure was happily rendered unnecessary by an agreement that Hon. Geo. F. Hoar be named as Chairman of the Convention, and that the question of enforcing the "unit rule" be postponed until after the report of the committee on credentials was in, when it could be settled in a regular way and in full convention. This plan of settlement was proposed by Chester A. Arthur of New York, who was afterward nominated for Vice-President.

Pursuant to this agreement, Senator Hoar was made temporary chairman, and afterward permanent chairman of the convention. Two days were consumed in getting the convention into working shape, such was the amount of friction between the contending parties and so anxious was each for vantage ground. On the third day, Mr. Conkling moved that each delegate pledge himself to support the nominee of the convention. This motion was carried almost unanimously, only a few delegates from West Virginia voting in the negative. Mr. Conkling immediately moved that they be expelled. This gave rise to a heated debate, which was terminated by the withdrawal of the motion by Mr. Conkling, at the pacific suggestion of Mr. Garfield. In the evening a spirited debate arose over the admission of the Alabama delegation, in which the point involved was the right of representation

WALTER DAMROSCH.

by districts or by States. The vote stood 449 for district representation, and 306 against. This settled the fate of the "unit rule" in the convention, and was a decisive defeat for the Grant forces.

The fourth day of the convention found the delegates weary by reason of the long continued excitement. They, however, received the report of the committee on Rules which disapproved of the unit system. The platform was also reported and adopted. The evening session was devoted to placing candidates in nomination. Mr. James F. Joy, of Michigan, placed the name of James G. Blaine in nomination, in a speech which fell far below the occasion. It was ably seconded by Mr. Pixley of California and Mr. Frye, of Maine. Mr. E. F. Drake, of Minnesota, presented the name of Mr. Windom, of that State. Senator Conkling presented the name of General Grant, in an eloquent address, which was seconded by Mr. Bradley, of Kentucky. General Garfield presented the name of Senator John Sherman of Ohio. Mr. Billings presented the name of Senator Edmunds of Vermont. Mr. Cassidy of Wisconsin presented the name of Hon. E. B. Washburne, of Illinois.

On the following Monday the Convention Hall was filled to overflowing with an audience whose sympathies were ready to run riot at mention of the names of favorites. Ten ballots were cast during the day. The Grant strength wavered between 303 and 308. The Blaine strength fluctuated from 280 to 284. The balloting was continued during the evening, and so on, until the thirty-sixth, and decisive one, no material change being perceptible until the thirty-fourth, when Garfield received

CHAPTER XVI.

AS SECRETARY OF STATE.

In making up his cabinet and with deference to all the political conditions, President Garfield could hardly refuse to select Mr. Blaine as his confidential advisor. He accordingly appointed an interview in Washington on Nov. 24, 1880, and tendered the Department of State to Mr. Blaine. Acceptance was deferred until Mr. Blaine became better acquainted with the sentiment such an offer was sure to evoke. In December the fact of the tender became public and began to draw most favorable discussions. This induced Mr. Blaine to accept the proffered honor, and on Dec. 20, 1880, he addressed Garfield thus:

WASHINGTON, D. C., Dec. 20, 1880.

MY DEAR GARFIELD:—Your generous invitation to enter your cabinet as Secretary of State has been under consideration for more than three weeks. The thought had really never occurred to my mind until at our late conference you presented it with such cogent arguments in its favor and with such warmth of personal friendship in aid of your kind offer.

I know that an early answer is desirable, and I have waited only long enough to consider the subject in all its bearings, and to make up my mind definitely and conclusively. I now say to you, in the same cordial spirit in which you have invited me, that I accept the position.

It is no affectation for me to add that I make this decision not for the honor of the promotion it gives me in the public service, but because I think I can be useful to the country and to the party; useful to you as the responsible leader of the party and the great head of the government.

I am influenced somewhat, perhaps, by the shower of letters I have received urging me to accept, written to me in consequence of the mere unauthorized newspaper report that you had been pleased to offer me the place. While I have received these letters from all sections of the Union, I have been especially pleased and even surprised at the cordial and widely extended feeling in my favor throughout New England, where I had expected to encounter local jealousy and perhaps rival aspiration.

In our new relation I shall give all that I am and all that I can hope to be freely and joyfully to your service. You need no pledge of my loyalty in heart and in act. I should be false to myself did I not prove true both to the great trust you confide in me and to your own personal and political fortunes in the present and in the future. Your administration must be made brilliantly successful and strong in the confidence and pride of the people, not at all directing its energies for re-election, and yet compelling that result by the logic of events and by the imperious necessities of the situation.

To that most desirable consummation I feel that, next to yourself, I can possibly contribute as much influence as any other one man. I say this not from egotism or vain glory, but merely as a deduction from a plain analysis of the political forces which have been at work in the country for five years past, and which have been significantly shown in two great National Conventions. I accept it as one of the happiest circumstances connected with this affair that in allying my political fortunes with yours—or rather for the time merging mine in yours—my heart goes with my head, and that I carry to you not only political support but personal and devoted friendship. I can but regard it as somewhat remarkable that two men of the same age, entering Congress at the same time, influenced by the same aims and cherishing the same ambitions, should never, for a single moment in eighteen years of close intimacy, have had a misunderstanding or a coolness, and that our friendship has steadily grown with our growth and strengthened with our strength.

It is this fact which has led me to the conclusion embodied in this letter; for however much, my dear Garfield, I might admire you as a statesman, I would not enter your cabinet if I did not believe in you as a man and love you as a friend.

Always faithfully yours,

JAMES G. BLAINE.

This was Mr. Blaine's acceptance, this his pledge of fidelity. Hardly anything could have been more in accord with his own exalted views nor more pleasing to the nation. Having entered his solemn compact, he resigned his seat in the senate and took his seat in the Garfield Cabinet, March 4, 1881. The Cabinet consisted of James G. Blaine, Secretary of State; William Windom, Secretary of the Treasury; Wayne McVeagh, Attorney General; Robert T. Lincoln, Secretary of War; Wm. H. Hunt, Secretary of the Navy; Samuel L. Kirkwood, Secretary of the Interior; Thomas L. James, Postmaster General.

The Cabinet was regarded as strong, and the government seemed to respond to the new hands at the helm. It was felt that the easy going policy of President Hayes would soon be replaced by something calculated to inspire greater confidence and contribute more to national dignity. The change was most agreeable, and visions were cherished which embraced the enlargement and glory of our institutions. The personal influence of Mr. Blaine was felt in all departments, but especially in the shaping of a foreign policy, in which his advice was largely deferred to.

The Senate was convened in extra session, in pursuance of a proclamation issued by President Hayes, on March 4, 1881. The parties were evenly divided, and no business of a party nature could be done without the aid of the casting vote of the President of the body. The appointment of cabinet officers was confirmed. The auspicious opening of the new Administration was marred by the intensification of factional differences, occasioned by President Garfield's New York appointments. On March 23, he sent in a large number of nominations among which was that of William H. Robertson, the leader of the Blaine wing of the Republican party in New York, to be Collector of Customs. He had previously sent in five names for prominent places in New York, at the suggestion of Senator Conkling, who had been invited by President Garfield to name his friends. At this interview it was stated that Garfield casually intimated that he would make no immediate change in the New York Collectorship, and both factions seemed satisfied to allow General Edwin A. Merritt to retain that place for a time at least. There were loud protests, however, at the first and early selection of the friends of Senator Conkling to five important places, and these protests were heeded by the President. With a view to meet them, and doubtless, to quiet the spirit of faction rapidly developing between the Grant and anti-Grant elements of the party in New York, the name of Judge Robertson was sent in for the Collectorship. He had battled against the unit rule at Chicago, disavowed the instructions of his State Convention to vote

XVII.

CONVENTION AND CAMPAIGN OF 1884.

THOUGH the Arthur administration had done much to remove the gloom occasioned by the assassination of Garfield and to soften the asperities that divided the Republican ranks in 1882–83, and led to the defeat of the party in most of its State elections, there was still considerable factional feeling as the political situation of 1884 took shape. But as time progressed and sentiment began to chrystalize, nothing seemed to shake the firm hold Mr. Blaine had on the affection of his friends. He had carried into private life all of his well-merited political renown, all his unequalled reputation for learning and eloquence, all the just confidence which had come to be reposed in his rectitude, all of the respect which a generous and loving people graciously extended to conscientious conduct and bravery of heart. And these were to grow as well in the shades of private retreat as in the sunshine of public life. Yea, faster and more luxuriantly, for there were now no dangers and embarrassments to encounter. The people were in a calm season of reflection. They could study and accord merit dispassionately. They could see strength and availability much clearer than when the atmosphere was beclouded with factional smoke.

And again, retiracy with Mr. Blaine, did not mean inaction and desuetude. He could not, if he would, lose his interest in the body politic nor in the welfare of his party. The mildew of retiracy could not settle on such an organization as his. He could not be idle. It would seem as if no public question escaped him. Not content with surface examination nor passing comments he sought the roots of pending questions, and whenever opportunity offered or occasion required, he wrote and spoke learnedly, lucidly and exhaustively. There was no obscuration of his genius by retiracy, no forgetfulness of his greatness by privacy. On the contrary, there was a daily growing admiration for his sterling qualities of head and heart, tinged, perhaps with regret that his country and party should not be all the while receiving the direct stimulus of his leadership and the immediate benefits of his ripened experience. The processes were silently at work deep down among the masses of his party, whose manifestation took the form of a resolve that he should be further honored by them with their greatest and best gift.

True, he was to be again an object of attack by his enemies, but their weapons would now fly far over his head. He was a private citizen, and attacks of any kind were both needless and wanton. Moreover, they assumed old and exploded forms, and became conspicuous only for sheer maliciousness, contributing more to the disgrace of their authors than to the injury of their object. They generally proceeded from a source outside of his party, and proved "stale, flat and unprofitable." There was, however, an element within the Republican party which stubbornly refused to yield to the element which shaped toward the nomination of Mr. Blaine for the presidency. It was that element which chrystalized under the leadership of Senator Edmunds of Vermont, and which, at first, simply demanded independence of party machinery, but which afterward switched off into the channels of "Free

Trade" and that indefinite doctrine which became known as "Mugwumpery."

As to Mr. Blaine's retiracy from public life, it was complete in so far as inclinations for the presidency were concerned. From the date of his retirement he gave no indication of a preference in that direction, on the contrary, he persistently refused to yield his consent to become a candidate, although often importuned to do so. He clung to this determination with Spartan firmness. To every solicitation his one answer was, "Gentlemen, I am not a candidate, and shall do nothing personally to promote my nomination." By this it must not be understood that he was not aware of the political situation. In fact he understood it thoroughly. The party need was a broad, pronounced, and as nearly unanimous sentiment as possible. Personalism was to be eliminated. The logic of the situation pointed to a man, but the man could not point to it. Yet he could no more stay it than could Canute the waves of the sea. The unit rule was a thing of the past in Republican National Conventions. The people were free in their Congressional districts to make their choice of delegates, and "district representation" was a living principle of the party. Blaine was the best known man in his party. He represented most completely its dominant thoughts. He was the chief centre of its confidences, the most perfect embodiment of its hopes and ambitions, the fullest symbol of true American character. It was but natural that the Republican masses, influenced by anything but their sturdy convictions, should spontaneously turn to one whom they knew so well and trusted and honored so highly. It was equally natural that they should transfer their rejoicings over their own freedom to rejoicings over the prospect of securing his nomination and to applause at the thing accomplished.

Walker Blaine.

CHAPTER XVIII.

THE CITIZEN STATESMAN.

THE result of the election of 1884 was not a defeat for Mr. Blaine, whatever it may have been for his party. His disappointment was keen, but not more so than would have been that of any other spirited man. It was aggravated by the fact that victory had been wrenched from him by the narrowest of all margins and by processes not beyond suspicion. Yet in all history never had self been so estranged from results. Tilden, in 1876, and for far less cause, had brought the corruptive influences of money and stealth to his vindication. Blaine acquiesced, knowing that office was no personal loss, and that his party was in no mood to claim honors by a second, and prolonged, contest.

He therefore fell naturally, if regretfully, into private life. But it was not inactive. In many respects it was most active. In not a few respects it was the most resplendent of the great man's career. The giant in repose was equal to tasks which the giant in action could not have accomplished. The calmness and meditation of a private hour resulted in an activity which transformed the statesman into the historian and gave to the nation and the world almost the equivalent of such an administration as might have been expected, had he been elected.

In its place, allusion has already been made to the publication of Blaine's renowned work, "*Twenty Years in Congress.*" This was the crowning feature of that leisure

CHAPTER XVIII.

THE CITIZEN STATESMAN.

THE result of the election of 1884 was not a defeat for Mr. Blaine, whatever it may have been for his party. His disappointment was keen, but not more so than would have been that of any other spirited man. It was aggravated by the fact that victory had been wrenched from him by the narrowest of all margins and by processes not beyond suspicion. Yet in all history never had self been so estranged from results. Tilden, in 1876, and for far less cause, had brought the corruptive influences of money and stealth to his vindication. Blaine acquiesced, knowing that office was no personal loss, and that his party was in no mood to claim honors by a second, and prolonged, contest.

He therefore fell naturally, if regretfully, into private life. But it was not inactive. In many respects it was most active. In not a few respects it was the most resplendent of the great man's career. The giant in repose was equal to tasks which the giant in action could not have accomplished. The calmness and meditation of a private hour resulted in an activity which transformed the statesman into the historian and gave to the nation and the world almost the equivalent of such an administration as might have been expected, had he been elected.

In its place, allusion has already been made to the publication of Blaine's renowned work, "*Twenty Years in Congress.*" This was the crowning feature of that leisure which followed his defeat of 1884. It was no less a substantial gift to the nation than a superb contribution to political literature. In itself it was sufficient to establish the fame of the writer, not only as an omnicient observer but as a conscientious preserver of vital facts.

The first volume of Mr. Blaine's "Twenty Years in Congress" appeared in 1884, and the second volume in 1885. The style of writing, aside from that of its politico-historic merits, is peculiarly that of the author—lucid, fair, racy; statesman, historian and editor, in happy combination. No other work embraces so full and impartial a review of the material and political life of the nation from 1860 to 1880 as this. It instantly attracted the wide attention at home which it deserved, and equally drew foreign attention. The London *Times* said of it:—"It is in no sense a party manifesto, but a careful narrative; popular, but not undignified in style, and remarkably fair and moderate in tone. He has expressed a decided opinion on all issues involved in the civil war, but he is able to appreciate the arguments and respect the motives of those he holds to have been most widely mistaken."

Such volumes as Mr. Blaine's "Twenty Years in Congress," may be left to speak for themselves. Were it not for the evidence of versatility and power they furnish, they might well pass as an episode in the life of one so distinguished in other fields of activity. When, however, they are followed, as they were, by another volume, in 1887, the claims of literary taste and the ambitions of authorship enter as essential factors into that fame which they could with difficulty augment. The year 1887 witnessed the publication of Mr. Blaine's "Political Discussions," a work which embraced his most important political, and other, utterances. This work will come to possess more and more value as time rolls on, for it not only contains the evidences of what Mr. Blaine most prized among his forensic, legislative and diplomatic efforts, but the student of his character will find in it that versatility of genius, that wonderful command of language, that exhaustive research, that magnificent marshalling of facts, that convincing logic, which gave to Blaine's speeches and writings a virility and popularity surpassed by no other statesman.

Mr. Blaine's retiracy meant the giving up, for a time, his Washington mansion on Jackson Square, near the White House. He had moved to this more subdued but elegantly appointed home from his own larger and more ostentatious mansion on Dupont Circle, whose capacity he had found to be greater than his needs, and the expense of maintaining which was more than he felt he could afford.

He withdrew from the National capital entirely and found the rest and privacy he required at his home in Augusta, Maine, and at his summer residence at Bar Harbor, on the Atlantic coast. All the conditions here conspired which were necessary for the completion of those literary labors which were to add so largely to his reputation.

The course of President Cleveland's administration and the general trend of public events had no keener observer and student than Mr. Blaine, during the period of his retiracy. He kept himself abreast of political events and in close touch with the mighty constituency of the land, whose allegiance was love and admiration, and which yearned for another opportunity to pay tribute to his broad qualifications and exalted name.

The great need of the Democratic party was something beyond the common-place which characterized the first two years of the Cleveland administration. Though Mr.

Cleveland had repeatedly declared, in public speech and writing, against a second term for a President, he could no longer conceal his ambition to succeed himself, and in throwing off the disguise, the need of an issue to attract attention to himself and to promote party cohesion became all the more imperative. This issue he sought in his celebrated message to the Fiftieth Congress, Dec. 5, 1887.

It was a brief paper of 4,500 words, and was a new departure in the way of annual messages. It made no allusion to matters of public concern as found in the reports of the various heads of departments, nor to any matter of general moment, except that branch of finance which embraced taxation, customs, duties and the surplus in the Treasury. In this respect it was a special and partisan plea for definite legislature during the session. It was far removed from the position assumed by Mr. Cleveland in his former messages, and was the confession of a convert to the free-trade doctrines maintained by a majority of his party. The message was a surprise to all except the initiated. It was accepted by the Democratic leaders as a timely declaration of the issues which would enter into the next campaign, with Mr. Cleveland as their exponent. The protection Democrats regarded it as an unwise paper, and one containing the elements of sure disaster. The Republicans treated it as a direct challenge to contest the case of Free-trade vs. Protection. They criticised it for its lack of new and convincing argument; its discrimination against the protective system in general, and the item of wool in particular; its unnecessarily narrow and bitter spirit, as evinced in such expressions as:—" But our present tariff laws, the vicious, inequitable and illogical source of unnecessary taxation, ought to be at once revised and amended. They looked upon it as disingenuous, illogical

Cleveland had repeatedly declared, in public speech and writing, against a second term for a President, he could no longer conceal his ambition to succeed himself, and in throwing off the disguise, the need of an issue to attract attention to himself and to promote party cohesion became all the more imperative. This issue he sought in his celebrated message to the Fiftieth Congress, Dec. 6, 1887.

It was a brief paper of 4,500 words, and was a new departure in the way of annual messages. It made no allusion to matters of public concern as found in the reports of the various heads of departments, nor to any matter of general moment, except that branch of finance which embraced taxation, customs, duties and the surplus in the Treasury. In this respect it was a special and partisan plea for definite legislature during the session. It was far removed from the position assumed by Mr. Cleveland in his former messages, and was the confession of a convert to the Free-trade doctrines maintained by a majority of his party. The message was a surprise to all except the initiated. It was accepted by the Democratic leaders as a timely declaration of the issues which would enter into the next campaign, with Mr. Cleveland as their exponent. The protection Democrats regarded it as an unwise paper, and one containing the elements of sure disaster. The Republicans treated it as a direct challenge to contest the case of Free-trade vs. Protection. They criticised it for its lack of new and convincing argument; its discrimination against the protective system in general, and the item of wool in particular; its unnecessarily narrow and bitter spirit, as evinced in such expressions as:—"But our present tariff laws, the vicious, inequitable and illogical source of unnecessary taxation, ought to be at once revised and amended. They looked upon it as disingenuous, illogical

General U. S. Grant.

Chester A. Arthur.

NATIONAL CAPITAL, WASHINGTON, D. C.

Rutherford B. Hayes.

Emmons Blaine.

BLAINE'S HOME AT WASHINGTON.

Roscoe Conkling.

BENJAMIN HARRISON.

Blaine in 1876.

Hon. John Sherman.

JAMES A. GARFIELD.

Gen. John A. Logan.

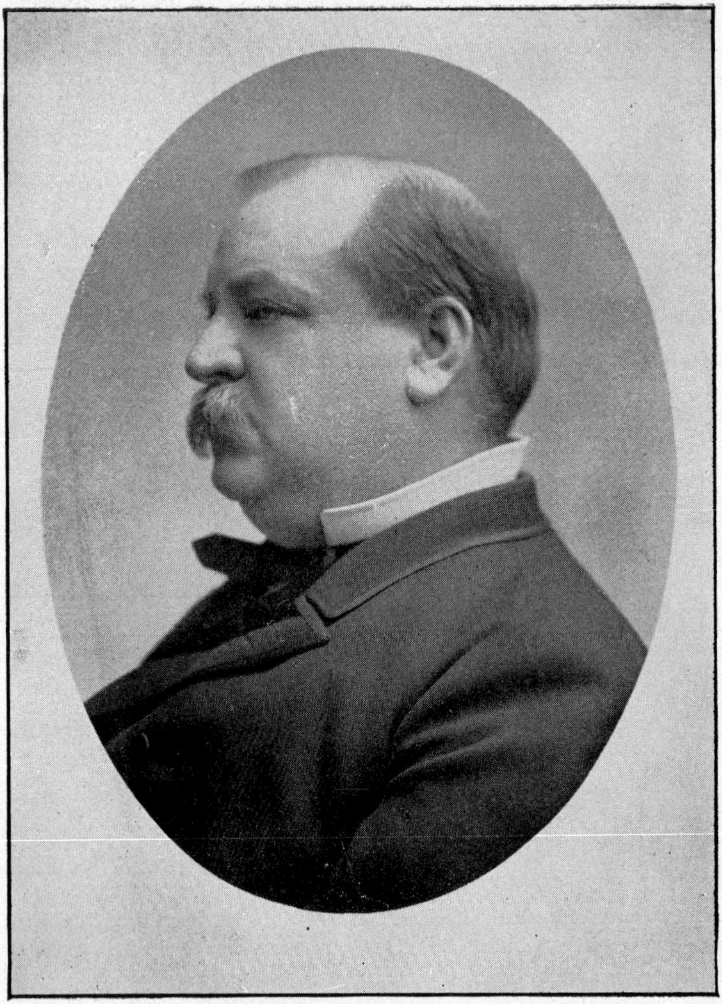

GROVER CLEVELAND.

Home of the Blaines at Bar Harbor, Me.

Harrison and Blaine Group at Bar Harbor.

On December 7, 1887, the London correspondent of the New York *Tribune* called on Mr. Blaine in Paris, to seek his views of the President's message, which had been cabled and published in the foreign papers, as significant of a new departure in the financial policy of the United States. Mr. Blaine assented to an interview, which was carefully noted by an expert stenographer. He began by saying:

"I have been reading an abstract of the President's message and have been especially interested in the comments of the London papers. Those papers all assume to declare that the message is a free trade manifesto, and evidently are anticipating an enlarged market for English fabrics in the United States as a consequence of the President's recommendations. Perhaps that fact stamped the character of the message more clearly than any words of mine can."

"You don't mean actual free trade without duty?" queried the reporter.

"No," replied Mr. Blaine. "Nor do the London papers mean that. They simply mean that the President has recommended what in the United States is known as a revenue tariff, rejecting the protective feature as an object and not even permitting protection to result freely as an incident to revenue duties. I mean, that for the first time in the history of the United States the President recommends retaining the internal tax in order that the tariff may be forced down even below the fair revenue standard. He recommends that the tax on tobacco be retained, and thus that many millions annually shall be levied on a domestic product which would far better come from a tariff on foreign fabrics."

"Then do you mean to imply that you would favor the repeal of the tobacco tax?"

CHAPTER XIX.

AGAIN SECRETARY OF STATE.

As the time for holding the Republican National Convention of 1888 drew near, a very pronounced element of the party, and a majority outside of the leaders, looked to Mr. Blaine as a certain candidate. True, he was absent from the country, and had been for some time, but distance had not diminished that popular esteem which welled spontaneously from the bosoms of his admirers. True, he had lost by time and distance those little intimacies and minor affiliations which count for so much among politicians when personal ambitions are to be served or where lines of candidature are to be established in advance. True, also, it had been given out that Mr. Blaine was averse to a nomination. The latter story was credited to the imagination of his opponents. Everything else, hostile to the thought and desire of his nomination, was cast aside by his friends, or securely buried beneath the reasons which moved them to demand his nomination. His reverses had intensified their determination to stand by him. The tantalizing results of 1884 called for another trial, and especially since everything pointed to the re-nomination of Cleveland, his old antagonist. The spirit of revenge burned within the breasts of those who had felt the dissappointments of that doubtful battle, far more than Mr. Blaine himself had done. The issues were those which were best calculated to call forth that championship of which Mr. Blaine was master. For these, and all other considerations, Mr. Blaine was not only a favorite, but a choice, far in advance of the Convention. He was, with his friends, the logical, the only candidate. They admitted no questions of expediency into their reasonings, and refused to modify the warmth and steadfastness of their support by anything which ran counter to their wishes.

Mr. Cleveland was nominated on June 5, at St. Louis. The Oregon State election had been fought on the issues contained in Cleveland's message of 1887, and the Republicans had gained an overwhelming victory. This served to freshen the Blaine reply to the message and to intensify the desire to see him pitted directly against the great modern exponent of free trade.

Both the friends and opponents of Mr. Blaine admit the impossibility of doing historic justice to his great name, during the year 1888, through use of the literature which constituted the rumors and passions of the hour There was no serenity of the party mind, no calm judgments of the events which involved Mr. Blaine's character and political fortunes. Dispassionate history may come to look on him as the victim of his friends, not intentionally of course, but through excess of enthusiasm, through disrespect of conditions which Mr. Blaine could, from his remote standpoint, weigh more deliberately than any one else. Even at this early date, it is not to be doubted that Mr. Blaine's physical condition was overlooked by his admirers, and that much of his reluctance to assume the responsibilities of a campaign and of office was due, not perhaps so much to actual disease, as to the dread of permanent impairment of a system already taxed to the uttermost by overwork, and so highly organized as to make it extremely sensitive to its environment. It is equally certain that there were other considerations operating with Mr. Blaine, no one of which might have been sufficient to induce him to decline a nomination, but whose cumulative effect he could not ignore. Any and all of said reasons he was under no obligation to explain. Indeed he could not have explained them with any sense of propriety, for, as with the question of health, that was a removable obstacle, and as to all other matters, he could have taken no pride in pandering to idle inquiry or curiosity.

Mr. Blaine had the reasons which weigh with great men for his attitude toward his friends and his party during 1888. These were sufficient for him. At the very beginning of the year, when party sentiment began to shape in his favor, he wrote home what became known as his "Florence Letter," with a view to keeping his name out of political controversy, and to letting sentiment take that natural direction toward candidates, which it might not otherwise do. With any other man, or at any other time, such a letter would have served the purposes of the writer. But in this instance it failed entirely of its object, and almost seemed to inflame the wishes and intentions it was designed to stifle. It ran as follows:—

FLORENCE, Jan. 25, 1888.—Mr. B. F. Jones, Chairman Republican National Committee—SIR: I wish through you to state to the members of the Republican party that my name will not be presented to the National Convention called to assemble in Chicago in January next for the nomination of President and Vice-President of the United States. I am constrained in this decision by considerations entirely personal to myself, of which you were advised more than a year ago. But I cannot make this announcement without giving expression to my deep sense of gratitude to the many thousands of my countrymen who have sustained me so long and so cordially with their feelings, which seemed to go beyond the ordinary political adherence of fellow partisans and to partake somewhat of the nature of personal attachment. For this most generous loyal friendship I can make no adequate return, and shall carry the memory of it while life lasts.

JAMES. G. BLAINE.

As the date of the Convention approached, and the questions of candidature assumed shape, the friends of Mr. Blaine became more and more determined to present his name to the Convention. Confidence in their ability to nominate him led them to construe his letter as not absolutely conclusive, and to believe that he would not refuse a nomination if tendered to him with a flatter'ng degree of unanimity. Information of this state of affairs reached him at Paris in May 1888, and he wrote as follows:—

"PARIS, May 17, 1888.

"Hon. Whitelaw Reid, Editor New York *Tribune.*"

"DEAR SIR:—Since my return to Paris from Southern Italy, the 4th inst, I have learned (what I did not believe) that my name may yet be presented to the National Convention as a candidate for the Presidential nomination of the Republican party. A single phrase of my letter of January 25, from Florence (which was decisive of everything I had personal power to decide), has been treated by some of my most valued friends as not absolutely conclusive in ultimate and possible contingencies. On the other hand, there are some equally devoted and disinterested persons who have construed my letter (as it should be construed) to be an unconditional withdrawal of my name from the National Convention. They have, in consequence, given their support to eminent gentlemen who are candidates for the Chicago nomination, some of whom would not, I am sure, have consented to assume that position if I had desired to represent the party in the Presidential contest of 1888. If I should now, by speech, or by silence, by commission or omission, permit my name in any event to come before the convention, I should incur the reproach of being uncandid with those who have always been candid with me. I speak, therefore, because I am not willing to remain in a doubtful attitude. I am not willing to be the cause of misleading a single man among the millions who have given me their suffrage and their confidence. I am not willing that even one of my faithful supporters in the past should think me capable of paltering in a double sense with my words. Assuming that the Presidential nomination could by any possible chance be offered to me, I could not accept it without leaving in the minds of thousands of these men the impression that I had not been free from indirection, and therefore I could not accept it at all. The misrepresentations of malice have no weight, but the just displeasure of my friends I could not patiently endure. * * * * *

"JAMES G. BLAINE."

It is difficult to conceive of how ideas could have been clearer or language more emphatic. Yet with all this there were those who, with a strange fatuity, persisted in showing their friendship and love for him by urging his name on the convention and insisting that he should be nominated.

The Republican Convention met at Chicago, June 19, 1888. There were many aspirants for nomination in the field, among whom were John Sherman, Ohio; Chauncey M. Depew, New York; William Walter Phelps, New

Jersey; Walter Q. Gresham, Illinois; Benjamin Harrison, Indiana; William E. Allison, Iowa; Russel A. Alger, Mich.; and Edward A. Fitler, Pa. Notwithstanding this array of candidates and this adaptation to geography, and the varied interests of the party, and notwithstanding the letters conveying explicit information as to Mr. Blaine's attitude, a powerful contingent in the convention kept his name prominently before it, and every mention of it was the signal for pronounced applause. Not for six days did the idea dissipate among his friends that he could not be nominated in spite of himself, and that if nominated with any degree of acclamation he would decline to accept. It was thus that his friends virtually held the convention and insisted on the chances evoked by the use of his name.

The situation remained thus till June 25, when were read the following dispatches, following each other in such rapid succession as to lead to the inference that Blaine was thoroughly alarmed at the indiscretion of his friends:—

"EDINBURGH, June 24.—To Boutelle and Manley, Chicago.—Earnestly request my friends to respect my Paris letter. "JAMES G. BLAINE."

EDINBURGH, June 24.—To Boutelle and Manley, Chicago.—I think I have a right to ask my friends to respect my wishes and refrain from voting for me. Please make this and the former despatch public.

"JAMES G. BLAINE."

These dispatches at once clarified the political atmosphere, and the work of balloting began, but every ballot showed how loth Mr. Blaine's friends were to resign his name entirely. Even on the eighth, and final ballot, which nominated Benjamin Harrison, by 544 votes, Mr. Blaine received five votes.

Mr. Blaine acquiesced most cordially in the result of the convention. Harrison's nomination had been made possible by the Blaine forces, and Mr. Blaine was too much of a politician as well as too much a lover of Republican principles to cherish disappointment when it was apparent that party victory could only be assured by locating the candidates in the two doubtful States of Indiana and New York. Among the flood of congratulations which poured in upon Mr. Harrison, none were more hearty than those of Mr. Blaine, and no man entered more enthusiastically into the campaign nor indulged more sanguine hopes of victory at the polls.

It was August before Mr. Blaine returned from his European tour. On the tenth of that month he arrived in New York and was enthusiastically welcomed by his admiring countrymen. A vast parade was formed in his honor, and the metropolis gave itself up to an ovation such as it had not witnessed before. Throughout the many scenes and varied speeches, Mr. Blaine distinguished himself by a demeanor and a line of thought that typed his thorough Americanism and endeared him to every witness, irrespective of party. He struck with thunderous vigor the campaign key-note of protection, and embellished the stated arguments by the fresh observations made during his extended travels in Europe. Applause was accorded him at every scene, of which he was the centre. His trip from New York to Augusta was a continuous ovation. The cities along the route vied with each other in extending honors. His presence and voice seemed to thrill all who saw and heard, and his name imparted a glow of enthusiasm to the campaign.

After a few weeks of rest at his Augusta home he took

the field for his party and principles. He visited many cities and States, addressing audiences swollen beyond the capacity of ordinary chambers and halls. Many days brought forth two to three of his inimitable addresses, and each day seemed to add to the brilliancy and efficacy of his speech. His physical resource seemed to be as inexhaustible as his mental. Conviction entered the minds of all whose ears hearkened to his eloquence and logic. Blaine never was so effective as in this campaign. Self was eliminated. He spoke briefly and pointedly. His very presence was an argument. Eclat preceded and followed him. At no time in his career was Blaine greater, because never so intense and disinterested. The result of the campaign, the splendid victory of Harrison and the Republican party was as much due to Mr. Blaine as to any other one man. It was therefore fitting that fresh honors should fall in his way.

President Harrison tendered him the post of premier in his cabinet. In doing so, he not only accorded what was due, but met the universal wish of his party. It was to the incoming administration an assurance of attainment which could not be surpassed. It was to Mr. Blaine the revival of an opportunity which had been cruelly denied him when Garfield fell beneath the assassin's bullet.

Mr. Blaine found himself, March 4, 1889, under a President in whom he had faith, and at the head of a brilliant cabinet. He was the centre of unbounded confidence, and upon a scene he could not help but adorn. He at once gave to his office the ripeness of his experience and the vigor of his original powers. Many delicate questions had come over from the previous administration whose adjudication could not longer be postponed with credit to American diplomacy and national honor. Of these Mr. Blaine at once took vigorous grasp.

CHAPTER XX.

FINAL RETIRACY FROM PUBLIC LIFE.

As party sentiment began to shape for the presidential struggle of 1892, Mr. Blaine found himself in very much the position he was in prior to 1888. His friends were equally ardent in his behalf, equally confident of their ability to make him the nominee of the party, and equally assured of his triumph at the polls, if nominated. Now as then, Mr. Blaine was equally silent as to his aspirations, and equally free from the combinations and machinations which make for success before conventions.

But while this was true of a position as made for him by his admirers, the resemblance did not hold in other respects. Mr. Blaine was no longer in a foreign land, but upon the scene of political action. He was not only present in the country but an occupant of high office. He had added to the esteem in which he was held by an administration of the Department of State at once vigorous and brilliant. But he was an official incumbent, and his chief was a likely candidate for re-nomination. Any mention of Mr. Blaine's name in connection with the presidency, under the circumstances, could hardly be other than embarrassing. Most especially would embarrassment ensue if efforts in his behalf should take the shape of antagonism to the chances of his chief, to whom he was thoroughly loyal.

The call for the Republican National Convention was made in November 1891, and it was to meet in Chicago on

June 7, 1892. At the time of the call, the thought was well nigh unanimous that President Harrison would be the nominee of his party

But after the turn of the year 1892 it was made apparent that there were elements in the Republican party which were hostile to the administration. These elements had previously made their mutterings known, but not in such a way as to lead to the suspicion that an open declaration of war was intended. The first overt opposition appeared in the local conventions of Pennsylvania, called at an unusually early period and with the evident intention of taking a snap judgment on the situation. They reflected the sentiment of those whose reason for hostility was inability to control as much patronage as they thought they deserved.

At first no serious attention was paid to this peculiar, unnecessary and impolitic movement. But when it was taken up in other sections, as New York, Ohio, Iowa and the silver States, and when it threatened to become formidable if left to run riot, there came a time for consideration on the part of Mr. Harrison's friends.

Among these friends, President Harrison counted on none as more intimate and safe than Mr. Blaine. He was his premier, his bosom friend of State, the custodian of his official secrets, the spokesman of his policy. None felt keener than Mr. Blaine the embarrassment likely to follow the freedom with which his name was used for the purpose of shaping opposition to the administration. Poison was added to the shaft by the fact that none of his now avowed admirers had been his friends in former years, but, on the contrary, had been his most bitter enemies. An additional source of chagrin and danger lay in the fact that the leaders of the opposition had failed of that importance in their own States which was necessary to save their party from disaster.

Out of the situation, clear to even the uninitiated, grew a motive, all compelling on the part of Mr. Blaine, if his relationship to the administration was to be maintained. He undoubtedly weighed it well. His decision was that he could not be a candidate. He embodied this decision in the following letter to Chairman Clarkson:—

WASHINGTON, Feb. 6, 1892.

HON. J. S. CLARKSON,

Chairman Republican National Committee.

MY DEAR SIR:—

I am not a candidate for the Presidency, and my name will not go before the Republican National Convention for the nomination. I make this statement in due season. To those who have tendered me their support, I owe sincere thanks, and am most grateful for their confidence. They will, I am sure, make earnest efforts in the approaching contest, which is rendered especially important by reason of the industrial and financial policies of the government being at stake. The popular decision on these measures is of great moment and will be of far-reaching consequence.

Very sincerely yours,

JAMES G. BLAINE.

This letter was regarded as magnanimous by every one, without regard to politics, for it was written in face of the fact that a sentiment was crystalizing about the writer's name which might have made him an easy victor at Minneapolis. It was further regarded by friend and foe as exceedingly timely, for the reason that it would prove a bar to all further improper use of his name and would

CHAPTER XXI.

A NATION MOURNETH.

On Saturday evening, Jan. 7, 1893, the illness of Mr. Blaine assumed such an alarming form as to dispel all hope of recovery. His condition was that of syncope, due to heart-failure. His two physicians alternated at his bedside during the night, and they succeeded in restoring him only by means of the most powerful medicaments.

The family group, summoned hastily to the scene of sorrow, and composed of Mrs. Blaine, Miss Harriet Blaine, Mrs. Damrosch and child, and the children of Colonel Coppinger, anxiously awaited the result. At six o'clock in the morning, when the hour had arrived when he must respond to remedies or finally succumb, the minister, Rev. Dr. I. S. Hamlin, pastor of the Presbyterian Church of the Covenant, was sent for, who held family devotions.

On the morning of Jan. 8 the physicians authorized a bulletin, the first of significance since that of Dec. 17. That of Dec. 17 read:

"Mr. Blaine has been suffering for some time past with symptoms of impaired general health, but which did not clearly indicate the disease of any particular organ. Evidence of local organic disease has been manifested recently, and it is believed his present condition is due to this cause. While there is nothing in the disease to warrant the fear of any very rapid progress, he has shown within a month past more signs of serious illness than before. It is hoped that this aggravation may pass off, but no positive statement can now be made as to changes which may take place from day to day."

That of Jan. 8, 1893, read:

"Yesterday Mr. Blaine lost strength, but last night his weakness became more decided for a few hours, and he seemed in danger of a speedy termination. Since morning, however, he is somewhat stronger, and at the present moment shows more decided evidence of rallying. But no great hope can be felt unless the improvement shall become more marked than at present, and be continued for some hours. His present symptoms are connected with an irregular and feeble action of the heart."

The dispatches of Jan. 9 were to the following effect:

"The indications to-night are that ex-Secretary Blaine may live for some days. His physicians do not anticipate an immediate dissolution. His existence at the present moment is due to his great vitality and recuperative powers, which have surprised even his physicians. The strongest stimulants are administered to him when prostrated as he was yesterday, and they seem efficacious; at least he is pronounced better this evening than he has been for four days past, which would mean that he had gained the ground lost yesterday.

"While his condition is very much improved this evening, the family and friends take but little encouragement therefrom. Absolute recovery cannot be hoped for. Since the first bad attack last month the idea of taking the distinguished patient to some warmer and pleasanter climate seems to have been abandoned, and the developments in the past few days seem to exclude all hope of his ever leaving his sick-bed. This is the opinion of all who visit the family and are received on intimate terms.

"The physicians, of course, cling to the old idea that while there is a slight spark of life there is hope of sustain-

Mrs Chas Grant May 18, 1906
Mrs Loyd C. Westerman Nov. 5 1906.